HERBCRAFTS

HERBCRAFTS

PRACTICAL INSPIRATIONS FOR
NATURAL GIFTS, COUNTRY CRAFTS AND
DECORATIVE DISPLAYS

  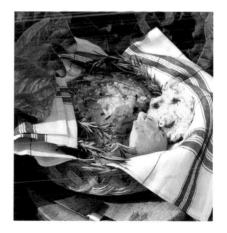

TESSA EVELEGH

PHOTOGRAPHS BY POLLY WREFORD

LORENZ BOOKS

LONDON • NEW YORK • SYDNEY • BATH

This edition published in the UK in 1997 by Lorenz Books

Lorenz Books is an imprint of
Anness Publishing Limited
Hermes House
88-89 Blackfriars Road
London SE1 8HA

This edition published in Canada by Lorenz Books, distributed by
Raincoast Books Distribution Limited, Vancouver

© 1997 Anness Publishing Limited

ISBN 1 85967 343 0

A CIP catalogue record for this book is available from the British Library

PUBLISHER: Joanna Lorenz
EDITORIAL MANAGER: Helen Sudell
DESIGNER: Prue Bucknall
PHOTOGRAPHER: Polly Wreford, additional photography by Michelle Garrett and Peter McHoy
STYLIST: Tessa Evelegh
ILLUSTRATOR: Michael Shoebridge

Printed and bound in Singapore

1 3 5 7 9 10 8 6 4 2

Contents

INTRODUCTION

Behind the lawn there may be great
diversity of medicinal and scented herbs,
not only to delight the sense of smell by
their perfume, but to refresh the sight with
the variety of their flowers.

The Secrets of Albertus Magnus,
Anon, Thirteenth Century

erbs have a magical quality. Locked into these modest-looking plants, which are commonly found in the hedgerows and meadows, is the power to heal and protect against disease, to provide delicious flavourings for food and perfume for the body. The plethora of books on the shelves bears witness to our love of herbs today. And yet, in centuries past, people were far more dependent on them than we are now, relying on all kinds of herbs for health itself.

Endowed with all these good qualities, herbs are truly a gift to us from Nature, all the more precious because their fragrance imparts a sense of well-being even in the healthy. To give herbs is to pass on to someone dear all the goodness that is locked within them, and that is the theme of this book. It contains a collection of lovely things to make and enjoy for yourself, or to give with love, offering with them a blessing of good health and happiness. None of the gifts is difficult to make or do and most are inexpensive. Some can even be made in batches. Delicate, fragrant, hand-made lavender moisturizer, for example, would be a treat for anyone, and you can make up a batch to be divided into

ABOVE *Stand herbs in plenty of cold water to keep them fresh before using.*

BELOW *Lavender is traditionally one of the most useful and versatile herbs for making gifts.*

several small but beautiful jars. Or buy some small herbs from a nursery or garden centre, then make up several baskets that can be given to grow and enjoy the whole summer through. You could make up several bottles of herbal oils and vinegars, too, to give and bring pleasure to friends over many meals.

Summer is the very best time to make herbal gifts, for this is when the herbs burgeon, growing at such a rapid rate, it seems, as to be able to offer the excess for our benefit. Early autumn is the time to use up the last of the summer herbs, before many varieties are cut back by the winter frosts, but even in winter there are dried herbs. By spring, it is time to think about making up growing herbal gifts.

Herbs are a joy to work with – their fragrance is delightful, and it can, in itself, be mood-enhancing and healing. I have enjoyed working on this book and through it, I hope, my love of herbs will bring hours of pleasure and enjoyment to others.

OPPOSITE *Growing your own herbs is a pleasure and means you can harvest as much as you need at your convenience.*

HERBAL HISTORY AND FOLKLORE

As for Rosmarine, it is the herb sacred to remembrance, and therefore, to friendship; whence a sprig of it hath a dumb language that maketh it the chosen emblem of our funeral wakes and in our buriall grounds.

SIR THOMAS MORE (1478-1535)

The many properties of herbs, used down the ages for medicinal and culinary purposes, have ensured them a place in human affections since pre-history. Herbs are nowadays treasured mainly for their culinary and horticultural uses, with a renewed and growing interest in medicinal and cosmetic aspects. For many centuries it was thought that they had magical powers. This is understandable: to the ancient mind the healing and protective properties of herbs must have seemed extraordinary. Lavender, for example, was carried by doctors visiting the sick, as it seemed to possess the power to guard against infection. We now know that lavender has antiseptic and anti-bacterial properties, and probably did provide protection.

ABOVE Fennel *by T. Sheldrake from the* Botanicum Medicinale *1759.*

Countless quaint ideas were recorded in herbals down the centuries. The eleventh-century *Herbarium of Apuleius* recorded:

For heart ache, take leaves of bramble, pounded by themselves; lay them over the left teat; the sore passes off.

and by the thirteenth century a group of Welsh physicians had found an unusual use for garlic:

Take a clove of garlic, prick it in three or four places, dip in honey and insert in the ear, covering with some block wool. Let the patient sleep on the other side every night, leaving the clove in the ear for seven or eight nights unchanged. It will prevent the running of the nose and restore the hearing.

However odd these ideas may seem to us nowadays, we still carry some of the legacy of the ancient beliefs in the magic of herbs. Rosemary was traditionally thought to ward off evil, and even now we consider it the herb of remembrance, possibly subconsciously recalling the "magic" of rosemary by sending off our dead under its protection. The other property of rosemary was as a matchmaker. Young girls, wishing to know who their future husbands were to be, were told to place a plate of flour under a rosemary bush at sunset on midsummer's eve. When they went to find the plate at sunrise, they would find the initials of their future love inscribed in the flour – the perfect opportunity, perhaps, for a keen young suitor to write in his own! But interwoven into herbals are remedies that worked for the ancients and still work for us.

The earliest known herbal is Chinese, said to have been written about 5,000 years ago by the legendary Emperor Shen Nung. Later, the ancient Egyptians used herbs to create exotic cosmetics and embalming lotions as well as remedies and flavourings. However, the first great breakthrough in herbal knowledge came in 60 AD when a Greek military doctor, Dioscorides, wrote about 600 plants in his *De*

ABOVE *An early illustration of sage from the* Tacuinum Sanitatum.

Materia Medica, which became a prime reference for future herbals for the next 1,500 years. The Romans spread herbal knowledge through Europe, but the decline of the Roman Empire heralded the Dark Ages, when the Christian Church frowned on scientific knowledge. At this time, Persia replaced Rome as the centre of learning, and Avicenna, a Persian physician, who gained some credit with discovering a way to distil essential oils, wrote *The Canon of Medicine* at the beginning of the second century.

Following that, most European herbals were written in Latin, mainly in Italy and Germany, representing facts from the original herbals, without adding new research.

The first original work in English did not appear until William Turner wrote *A New Herball* in 1551. A clergyman who travelled Europe researching the herbs for himself and studying under respected botanists in Italy and Germany, his herbal discounted many myths and superstitions. It brought a new enlightenment to those practitioners who, unable to read the original Latin herbals themselves, had had to rely on the sometimes doubtful herbal knowledge of the women who collected the herbs for apothecaries. The rather more popular herbal (*The Herball*) by John Gerard, a gardener who had access to an English translation of Latin material, was, regrettably, seasoned with extraordinary myths that discredited it amongst scientists of the day. This pattern was repeated in the next century, with John Parkinson's erudite *Theatrum Botanicum* of 1640 being followed by Nicholas Culpeper's dubious *The English Physitian* of 1653, in which bona fide knowledge was adulterated by folklore and astrology.

By the eighteenth century, the advance of modern science had eclipsed the proliferation of

ABOVE *A merchant selling thyme in a fifteenth-century translation of* Dioscorides' *herbal.*

herbals. Much later, however, a series of pamphlets, written by Maud Grieve, was collected into *A Modern Herbal* in 1931. Inspired by the herbals of old, it is a classic of its day, and includes detailed information about the cultivation and uses of herbs, as well as traditional anecdotes and folklore. As a piece of research it was respected by contemporary botanists and pharmacists, and its reissues, in 1973 and 1994, bear witness to the current resurgence of interest in all things herbal.

MEDICINAL HERBS

[THYME IS] A NOBLE STRENGTHENER OF THE LUNGS, AS NOTABLE A ONE AS GROWS, NOR IS THERE A BETTER REMEDY FOR HOOPING COUGH. IT PURGETH THE BODY OF PHLEGM AND IS AN EXCELLENT REMEDY FOR SHORTNESS OF BREATH.

NICHOLAS CULPEPER (1616-54),
THE ENGLISH PHYSITIAN

The herbs of the hedgerow were, until relatively recently, the people's medicine chest. Even in the early part of the twentieth century, herbs provided most remedies for all but the very rich, the doctor being far too expensive for the treatment of minor ailments. Nowadays, with easy access to synthetic drugs, the doctor's advice is sought even for temporary conditions. But there is a growing recognition that modern drugs are perhaps not the panacea we thought they were. A greater awareness of the long-term effects of some modern drugs is making us treat them with greater respect, often preferring to use them only when really necessary. Many continental European and Asian countries have kept the tradition of herbal healing alive, and now in Britain and America, too, people are returning to more natural remedies.

Many traditional herbal remedies evolved through a system of trial and error and recipes were passed down through the generations. Nobody really knew why they worked, and their qualities were often attributed to curious outside influences, such as astrology. Modern science has enabled the properties of herbs to be analysed, and has often isolated particular properties to be used in synthetic drugs. It is this isolation that marks the difference between herbal medicine and "orthodox" medicine.

Herbalists believe that the whole herb should be used, as some constituents of the plant may modify others, possibly making them more effective or less harsh. Herbalists aim for a balance within the body, to achieve a sense of well-being as well as good health. Their herbal remedies using whole plant material are easy for the body to digest and assimilate. They may take longer than "orthodox" medicine to have an effect, but the pace is one the body can cope with and it is less likely to over-react. However, just because they are natural does not mean herbs are not powerful. They should be used with care and, except for the most basic remedies, under the supervision of a herbal practitioner. Pregnant women should avoid all kinds of remedies – herbal as well as orthodox – unless under professional supervision. Also, some herbal remedies are muscle-stimulating, and can cause uterine contractions.

MAKING HERBAL REMEDIES

There are several ways to make use of herbs. It is best to use fresh herbs from a reliable source so you can be sure of the species of the plant. If you collect from the wild, use a botanical guide for correct identification. If you are at all unsure what the herb is, do not use it.

HERBAL INFUSION

This is a method of extracting the properties of the soft part of the herb, such as the leaves and flowers. An infusion is also called a tisane or tea.

Put 25 g/1 oz of the dried herb into a pot and pour 600 ml/1 pt/$2\frac{1}{2}$ cups boiling water over it. If using fresh herbs, use twice the weight of dried. Leave it to infuse for 10 minutes, then strain and drink one-third, reserving the rest for two further treatments. To make a single cup, pour 200 ml/$\frac{1}{3}$ pint boiling water on to 1 tsp of dried herbs.

HERBAL DECOCTION

Where the herb material to be used is hard – the roots or bark, for example – an infusion would not be able to extract enough of the properties. In this case, make a decoction.

Place 25g/1oz of the herb in a pan with 900ml/$1\frac{1}{2}$ pts/$3\frac{3}{4}$ cups of water and bring to the boil. Turn down the heat and simmer until the liquid has reduced to 600 ml/1 pt/$2\frac{1}{2}$ cups.

HERBAL COMPRESS

Soak a clean cotton cloth in a hot or cold herbal infusion or decoction. Squeeze out the excess liquid and apply to the affected area.

HERBAL POULTICE

Boil chopped fresh herbs for about five minutes. Strain them and squeeze out any excess liquid, then place them on the affected area and bind in place with gauze. Do not use on broken skin.

HERBAL STEAM INHALATIONS

Pour 600 ml/1 pt/2$\frac{1}{2}$ cups boiling water into a large bowl and add 300 ml/$\frac{1}{2}$ pt/1$\frac{1}{4}$ cups of herbal infusion. Lean over the bowl, place a towel over both your head and the bowl and inhale the steam.

ABOVE *Steam inhalations are an excellent way to clear the sinuses.*

RIGHT *A collection of dried herbs and flowers ready for use in herbal teas, infusions and decoctions.*

AROMATHERAPY

LAVENDER IS NOT ONLY SWEET OF SMELL,
AND THEREFOR COMFORTABLE TO THE BRAINE,
BUT ALSO GOOD FOR THE PALSIE AND ALL
OTHER INFIRMATIES.

THOMAS COGAN (c.1545-1607), THE HAVEN OF HEALTH

The powerful effect of aromas has long been valued: the ancient Egyptians, Romans and Persians became experts in making scented unguents and oils, and today we spend extraordinary amounts of money on perfumes. But wonderful aromas are more than a luxury: they can be used for healing and creating a sense of well-being. The ancients knew this, and burnt aromatic herbs to fumigate sick rooms. Indeed, the very word perfume comes from the Latin *per fume* ("through smoke").

Although the term "aromatherapy" was coined by René-Maurice Gattefosse only in 1920, the technique it describes has been used for centuries. In the third century BC, the Greek philosopher and botanist, Theophrastus, wrote about the healing effects of aromas in his book, *Concerning Odours*. Until relatively modern times, herbs were used for strewing, not only to sweeten the air in a room, but also, it was believed, to rid the area of infection.

HOW TO USE ESSENTIAL OILS

Essential oils are highly concentrated, and have to be used with great care. Only lavender oil and tea-tree oil can be used undiluted, and under no circumstances should any oil be consumed by mouth. Also, however much aromatherapy appeals, it should be avoided during pregnancy as some of the essences may stimulate contractions. Essential oils should not be used for children under two years old. For the rest of us, the oils can be used in several different ways.

IN A BURNER

Burning essential oils perfumes the air, often creating a sense of well-being. You will need a special burner which consists of a shallow bowl over a small chamber containing a night-light. Put a tablespoon of warm water in the bowl, add a few drops of essential oil, light the night-light, then sit back and enjoy! You will need to top up the water as it evaporates.

Once lit never leave the burner unattended, even for a few minutes, and never leave an unsupervised child in the room with it.

IN THE BATH

Relax in a scented bath and enjoy the soothing benefits offered by an added essential oil. The oil (no more than 10 drops) should be diluted in a little almond or other vegetable oil in a bowl before being added to the bath water as this will help to disperse it.

FOR MASSAGE

An essential oil blended with a carrier oil such as almond, wheatgerm or soya oil makes a perfect massage oil. Blend the oils in the proportion of 2-3 drops of essential oil to 1 tsp of carrier oil. For larger quantities, use 20-60 drops of essential oil to 100ml/3$^1/_2$ fl oz carrier oil.

AS AN INHALATION

Inhaling tiny droplets of essential oils into the lungs means they can be quickly absorbed into the bloodstream. Add six drops of essential oil to a bowl of steaming water. Lean over the bowl, with a clean towel covering your head and the bowl, and breathe in deeply through your nostrils.

ABOVE LEFT *A burner can quickly scent a room.*

OPPOSITE *Aromatherapy oils add wonderful scents to bathroom products.*

HERB GARDENS

Fragrant, delicious and a delight to the eye, herbs excite most of the senses, and this has ensured them a place as garden favourites for centuries. Much of the joy of a herb garden comes from the sheer pleasures of its beauty and its intoxicating perfume, and the cultivation of scented plants is a tradition that goes back many centuries. Our word "paradise" comes from the ancient Persian *pairidaezas*, walled scented gardens which included aromatic herbs. However, the delicious flavours these modest plants can offer mean that herb gardens are often kitchen gardens, too.

In centuries gone by, herb gardens were a much more serious affair than most are now. Grown for their medicinal and culinary properties, herbs were seen as virtually life-giving and almost magical. Traditionally, it was believed that herbal knowledge was revealed to a chosen few by angels and saints, and this was emphasized by the fact that for many centuries it was the monks who were the main guardians of herbal lore and herb gardening. Their gardens were strictly utilitarian, with a small rectangular

ABOVE *A blue herb garden can be wonderfully relaxing. This one is planted with French lavender, catmint in the background and violas in the urn.*

OPPOSITE *This glorious informal garden is focused by the bird bath and sundial as well as the criss-crossing pathways. The wisteria-hung pergola offers further structure. The herbs themselves are planted with contrasting colours placed cheek by jowl to set each other off – soft mauve against emerald and citrus against mint green.*

bed devoted to each herb and gravel paths between to make for easy tending.

After the dissolution of the English monasteries by Henry VIII early in the sixteenth century, herb gardens were released from the monks' care. From then on, they became far more decorative and soon knot gardens were developed. These consisted of simple geometric or curved patterns, interlinked to look like knotted twine, and outlined on the ground using low hedges of box, lavender, rosemary or cotton lavender. Various herbs or coloured shingles were used to fill in the shapes.

Europe, towards the end of the sixteenth century, saw a proliferation of scented herb gardens tended by the ladies of the largest houses. These often included flowers, such as roses, for purely decorative purposes. Knot gardens increased in complexity, and parterres, which consisted of a series of knot gardens, came to the fore. The seventeenth century saw the rise of the herbalists, and with them, the physic gardens. In contrast to the decorative gardens, these had a scientific purpose and supplied the needs of the apothecaries. But this was the heyday for herbs.

Later, as explorers and botanists thirsted for exotic finds in far continents, and medicine moved towards synthetic processes, herbs fell

OPPOSITE *Young standardized box plants provide the focal point for a wonderfully textural knot, with varieties of different shades offering extra depth to the design.*

out of favour. They came to be regarded as folk medicine and relegated to the country kitchen cupboard. It was not until the end of the nineteenth century, with the Arts and Crafts movement, that herbs began to be valued again and used in an informal decorative way.

For most of the twentieth century, gardening fashion has been for informal planting, though, as it draws to a close, formality is once more becoming the vogue. Both are charming, but, whichever you plan, aim to create some structure. A formal garden incorporates structure in its very form; an informal one will need the help of elements such as statuary, a bird bath, a sundial or even furniture, as well as the structure of paving or gravel paths, to pull your design together.

ABOVE LEFT *Gravel paths are traditional in herb gardens, providing practical and inexpensive access to a working area.*

FAR LEFT *All alliums make for spectacular planting. These Welsh onions have striking blue-green foliage topped by cheeky cream pom-poms.*

LEFT *Plant herbs in graduating heights in the borders, contrasting the colours for emphasis.*

HERBS TO GROW

ONCE HE HAS PREPARED THE SOIL, HE SOWS THE

SEEDS OF HERBS SUCH AS DILL AND CUMIN.

ISAIAH 28:25

Climate, Seeds and Cuttings

I HAVE LABOURED WITH THE SOILE TO MAKE IT FIT
FOR PLANTS AND WITH THE PLANTS, THAT THEY
MIGHT DELIGHT IN THE SOILE, THAT SO THEY
MIGHT LIVE AND PROSPER UNDER OUR CLYMAT, AS
IN THEIR NATIVE AND PROPER COUNTREY.

JOHN GERARD (1545-1612), THE HERBALL

Even outside their native lands, herbs are surprisingly hardy. Lavender and thyme, sage and oregano, all native to the countries bordering the Mediterranean, grow happily in more northern climes. Suited to a dry, hot climate, herbs do not expect a lot of watering, and do not need much fertilizing. However, that does not mean they can be ignored – the directory at the end of this book outlines the best conditions for growing the most popular herbs.

Herbaceous plants are defined as those that die down in the winter. Many of the plants that we describe as herbs – such as thyme, bay and lavender – do not do this, but there are many others that do and, when spring arrives, these put on astonishing growth. Large plants, such as angelica or globe artichokes, can easily grow to 2 m/6 ft. Most are not quite so dramatic, though summer growth is always

ABOVE *Collect your own seed or buy from the large range available in the shops.*

OPPOSITE *By late spring, when the frosts are over, the lid can be taken off the cold frame and the herbs can be hardened off and planted outdoors.*

BELOW *Take cuttings by removing young shoots near to a leaf node in late summer.*

rapid. If you keep your herbs in a container their growth will not be so abundant as they will not have access to as many nutrients as those growing in the open ground.

Herbs can be grown from seed or cuttings, or bought as young plants. Growing on plants from a nursery or garden centre is the easiest option, though taking cuttings is easy too, and costs almost nothing. Cuttings should be taken in early summer. Remove several shoots from the plant with a sharp knife and strip off the lower leaves. Dip the stems in rooting hormone and place them in pots of specially formulated cuttings compost. If the cuttings have taken, new shoots will begin to appear. Cuttings from woody-stemmed herbs can be taken in late summer. Keep the new plants in the greenhouse until the following spring when the frosts are over and they can be planted out.

You can collect your own seed by tying a paper bag over flowerheads that have gone to seed. However, a surer method is to buy seed. Sow it in trays of seed compost and cover them with newspaper until the seedlings appear. Thin if necessary, and when they are strong enough, prick them out. Fill small pots with compost, then lift the seedlings out of the seed tray, trying not to damage their roots. Make a hole in the compost using a dibber and plant the seedling. The plants should be strong enough to plant out by late spring when the frosts are over.

HARVESTING AND DRYING

NOW HOPPING IS ALL OVER, ALL THE
MONEY SPENT,
AND DON'T I WISH I'D NEVER GONE HOPPING
DOWN IN KENT.

TRADITIONAL SONG

Herbs are bountiful, putting on rapid growth during the summer months, so there is plenty to harvest for culinary use over the summer and an abundance in the autumn when the season is over. In fact, herbs benefit from a certain amount of harvesting during their growing period over the summer. It is best to keep pinching out the tops to encourage bushiness and to stop flowers from forming. Thus collecting herbs for the cooking pot can benefit the plant – provided you do not denude it. However, if you would like to enjoy the flowers on your herbs, allow some plants to bloom while pinching out others for use in the kitchen.

Herbs are best harvested in mid-morning, after the dew has dried but before the aroma has been dissipated by the hot sun. Use sharp secateurs, and, if you are harvesting during the growing season, aim to improve the shape of the plant by taking stems that have grown overlong. Herbs are lovely used fresh, and during the summer you will probably prefer to harvest just as you need them. By the beginning of autumn, the herbs are more or less over and will need to be cut down. This is the time for the major harvest. As you cut them, make them into small bunches using elastic bands. You can use string if you like, but elastic bands are better because they tighten round the herb stalks as they dry. The bunches should then be hung upside down to dry in a well-ventilated, damp-free room. As they dry, the herbs become more brittle, and this is the stage when you may like to make them into bouquet garnis, preserving all the tiny leaves until you are ready to use them in the cooking pot. Simply wrap up either a single variety or a selection of dried herbs into squares of muslin, then tie with cotton string.

LEFT *Hang your herbs upside down in a dry, airy place, out of direct sunlight. Once dry, wrap them up in plain brown paper*

RIGHT *Bay leaves dry very readily, retaining their shape well. They make delightful gifts when tied into bundles with raffia and packaged into miniature kilner jars.*

OPPOSITE *When the herbs are all gathered in, tie some into little bundles with raffia to use fresh as aromatic faggots. Others can be made into bunches using elastic bands, then hung up to dry.*

PLANTING A KNOT GARDEN

A small knot garden can provide a framework for a culinary herb plot, making a delightful feature within a larger garden. Planting one is not difficult to do, though the young box plants need time to grow to complete the framework. By the end of the second summer, however, the design should be filled in.

MATERIALS

GRAPH PAPER

PENCIL

DWARF BOX PLANTS (*Buxus sempervirens*) – ONE FOR EVERY 15 CM/6 IN OF OUTLINE

STAKES

GARDEN TWINE

SPADE

TOPIARY TREES: CHOOSE FROM BOX (*Buxus*) OR PRIVET (*Ligustrum*) FOR SMALL GARDENS

HERB PLANTS

OPPOSITE *Potted angelica plants provide detail in a simple but punchy knot garden. This is a useful trick which allows the pots to be exchanged for other plants as the year progresses.*

1 Work out a simple design to scale on graph paper, bearing in mind that the box hedging will be about 15 cm/6 in wide. Lay out the design on level ground, placing the plants about 15 cm/6 in apart. A rough calculation would be almost a hand span apart.

2 Once the outline is laid out, mark out the perimeter using stakes and twine, then dig the garden out. Reposition the box plants and plant them in position. Plant topiary trees to add interest and fill each section with herbs. Water the garden well for the first year until the plants have established. Trim the box hedges to shape twice a year: in midsummer and late autumn.

ABOVE *A simple knot garden formed by box hedging makes a delightful framework for a culinary herb garden. Plant a different herb in each section to create a living tapestry.*

ABOVE *As the tops of the young standard herbs grow, trim them to shape. This will probably be only once in the second summer.*

LEFT *Three young standard herbs, thyme, sage and rosemary, are beginning to take shape in their second summer, but still need the support of stakes. The sage is laden with large buds, which will open later into flamboyant blue flowers.*

STANDARD HERBS

The fashion for standardizing all manner of shrubs has extended to herbs, and this is a most charming way to grow them. Many herbs tend to grow into somewhat unruly bushes, but training them into standards changes their personalities and transforms them into enchanting little trees. This is particularly successful with herbs such as rosemary, which can grow into a large bush. By standardizing rosemary it can be tamed, making it an ideal solution in a small garden where space is at a premium.

You can only standardize the woody-stemmed herbs, such as thyme, sage, rosemary and lavender, and, unless you can buy them ready trained, you will need to be patient. It takes several years for the woody stem to grow strong enough to support the bushy top growth.

To train a standard, wait until the stems of the plant become woody and there is an obvious leader. Using a sharp pair of secateurs, trim off all the lower side shoots. Tie the stem to a bamboo stake, using soft string that will not damage it. Continue to trim off any side shoots that appear, and let the top develop. As the top grows, keep it trimmed to shape.

KITCHEN SILL
HERB GARDEN

Bring a little of the garden indoors by setting out a windowsill garden in the kitchen. You can use garden containers to recreate the outdoor feel, teaming an urn with clay pots, each planted up with an individual herb. Here, the lovely full shape of a strawberry plant perfectly complements the urn, though it may be grateful for some fresh air – you can open a nearby window, or you may like to put the plant outside at night occasionally in the summer. Thyme, marjoram, sage and comfrey fill a group of smaller pots, and globe artichokes complement the delicate colours of the herb flowers.

ABOVE *A delightful kitchen windowsill arrangement combines culinary herbs with purely decorative ones. The large pot has a strawberry plant in it and the small pots contain (from left to right) thyme, gold-tipped marjoram, sage and comfrey.*

ABOVE *The translucent flowers of comfrey look as if they have just been brought in from the hedgerow.*

HERBAL HANGING BASKET

Create a deliciously fragrant herbal hanging basket and suspend it outside the kitchen window, ready to use when needed. This one has been planted up in an old agricultural metal basket, but it would look equally pretty in a purpose-made hanging basket. Some yellow bidens is included for extra colour.

MATERIALS

SKEIN OF GREEN RAFFIA (OPTIONAL)

HANGING BASKET ABOUT 35 CM/14 IN DIAMETER

SHEET PLASTIC

TROWEL

CONTAINER COMPOST

4 VARIEGATED IVIES

VARIEGATED GOLDEN SAGE (*Salvia officinalis* 'ICTERINA')

CHAMOMILE (*Chamaemelum nobile*)

WILD STRAWBERRY (*Fragaria vesca*)

GOLDEN MARJORAM (*Origanum vulgare* 'AUREUM')

3 YELLOW *Bidens ferulifolia*

OPPOSITE *A herbal basket makes a thoughtful gift for keen cooks and gardeners. This one is planted in an agricultural basket, and the sides have been decorated by weaving in green raffia.*

1 Weave raffia around the sides of the basket to decorate it if you wish. Line the basket with sheet plastic and make some holes in the bottom for drainage. Put a 7.5 cm/3 in layer of compost in the bottom.

3 Add more compost to the basket until it is the correct depth for the sage and chamomile. Position these and add more compost until it is the correct depth for the rest of the plants.

2 Take one ivy from its pot, shake off any excess compost and feed the root through the struts of the basket. Thread the leaves in and out of the struts. Repeat with the other three ivies.

4 Add the rest of the plants. Push compost around each plant and add a fine layer on the top, pressing it down firmly. Allow a 2.5 cm/1 in space between the top of the compost and the rim of the basket for watering. Water when the compost feels dry and liquid-feed once a month.

GIFTS FOR GARDENERS

I t is wonderful to give growing gifts for exactly that reason – they get bigger. Even a packet of seeds holds such promise, and as plants burgeon they are a constant reminder of the giver. As with all gifts, presentation often counts as much as the gift itself, but that does not necessarily mean using fancy paper and ribbons. You could dress up herbs by planting them in a pretty container, add some twine or raffia for decoration, or tuck in some beautiful old tools, their handles polished with age.

OIL CAN HERB GARDEN

This witty presentation evokes salad dressing – colourful Mediterranean vegetable oil cans filled with the fresh herbs that go into salads. Once you have used the delicious oil they contain, use a can opener to remove the tops, drill drainage holes in their bases, varnish the cans with clear varnish to avoid rust developing and then simply plant up! Take care when planting as the tin edge is very sharp.

ABOVE *Plant up a kitchen garden in a selection of oil cans, choosing a variety of sizes for a better show. These have been planted up with (from left to right) marjoram, nasturtiums, parsley, sage and borage.*

A GIFT TO GROW

Even those who have everything will welcome a kit for growing herbs. There is a thrill to planting some improbably small seeds and then watching them sprout and grow. And since herbs grow so fast in the summer, they are immensely satisfying. The seeds should really be planted in early spring under glass so that they are well established by the time the frosts are over and they can go outside.

RIGHT *The patina of age bestows a great beauty on garden classics, and, put together thoughtfully, they can make a wonderful gift. Here, a traditional English garden basket, which can be used as a seed tray to germinate the seeds, becomes a container for the rest of the gift. Once they have sprouted, the seedlings can then be transferred to the old clay pots and left to grow in these all summer if desired*

HERB WINDOW BOX

Outdoor window boxes offer a decorative touch to both house and garden, and, if placed on a kitchen windowsill, the contents can be used for culinary purposes too. This arrangement is planted in an old fruit box that has been colour-washed to tone with the herbs. Borage has been included: while still rather small in early summer, it will shoot up into a stately plant with pretty pendulous blue flowers to provide interest later in the season.

1 Water the paint down until it is very thin to provide a translucent veil of colour over the box. The colour will last the summer through, and you can always repaint with another colour next year.

2 Line the box with sheet plastic and make holes in the bottom for drainage. Cover the plastic with a layer of container compost.

OPPOSITE *Scented geraniums and lavender provide colour and fragrance to this culinary window box.*

3 Arrange the plants in the box, placing the larger plants to the back, the smaller to the front. Remember that though the borage is small now, it will eventually become the largest plant.

4 Fill in with compost between and around each plant, bedding them in well. Add a final top layer and firm down. Water well, and afterwards water when the surface of the compost feels dry. Liquid-feed once a month.

THYME POT

A cross between a herb pot and a thyme garden, this makes a charming gift. Thyme comes in such an enormous range of colours and textures that a pot like this can become something of a herbal sampler, becoming fuller as the summer progresses. Thyme is also a very useful flavouring for meat dishes.

MATERIALS

CROCKS
HERB POT ABOUT 25 CM/10 IN HIGH
CONTAINER COMPOST
TROWEL
Thymus 'PORLOCK'
Thymus 'HIGHLAND CREAM'
Thymus x *citriodorus* 'AUREUS'
Thymus x *citriodorus* 'SILVER QUEEN'
GOLDEN THYME (*Thymus vulgaris aureus*)

OPPOSITE *Make up a thyme pot at the beginning of summer and watch it grow over the season. Thyme is a perennial, so keep up the watering over the winter and you'll be rewarded with another show next year.*

1 Place crocks over the drainage hole in the bottom of the herb pot.

2 Put a layer of compost in the bottom of the pot until it reaches the level of the first hole.

3 Saving the 'Porlock' for the top, remove one of the other thymes from its pot and shake off any excess compost. Gently feed it through one of the holes. Add compost, bedding the plant in well. Continue to add compost until it reaches the level of the next hole. Repeat with another thyme.

4 Finally, plant the 'Porlock' in the top of the pot, add more compost around the edges, and bed it in firmly. Water well. Once planted, water when the top of the compost feels dry to the touch.

DECORATIVE HERBS

NOSE-GAIES AND POSIES, WHICH ARE DELIGHTFUL TO
LOOKE ON AND PLEASANT TO SMELL TOO, SPEAKING
NOTHING OF THEIR APPROPRIATE VERTUES.

JOHN GERARD, THE HERBALL, 1597

The charm of herbs lies in their modesty. Since scent, taste and medicinal properties are herbs' raison d'etre, horticulturalists have found no need to develop hybrids with showy blooms. Gaudy ostentation simply is not the style of herbs, and the end result is delightful plants that look as if they have been picked wild from the hedgerows and meadows. And as they put on astonishing growth every summer, there is usually plenty to be harvested from the herb garden for decorative purposes.

Gather a large bunch to put in a vase or jug for a fuss-free yet wonderful display, or follow an ancient tradition and make charming little tussie mussies (aromatic posies) to give as gifts or place in a vase at home. Set one on a guest's bedside table for decorative appeal and lend fresh seasonal fragrance to the room.

Herbs can also be used for more elaborate decorative purposes: to make wreaths, garlands and faux topiary. As well as being attractive to look at, their distinctive aroma adds to the ambience. It is best if you can fix the stalks into soaked florist's foam, which will keep the arrangement looking fresh for days. Afterwards, you can remove the herbs, snip off the ends of

ABOVE *Containers, wires, florist's foam, secateurs and plenty of fresh herbs make up the main ingredients for fresh displays.*

OPPOSITE *Honeysuckle and roses make a delightful perfumed posy.*

BELOW *Lavender, oregano and marjoram are three of the most useful herbs for decorative arrangements.*

the stalks and hang them up to dry for future use. If it is not possible for the herbs to be in water, choose the woodier varieties, such as rosemary and bay, which will retain their freshness for longer.

By their very nature, many herbs are small-leaved and have small flowers, and to create impact it is best either to use just one, with perhaps another decorative one for interest, or to group them, working in sections of different varieties.

When they dry, many herbs shrivel to almost nothing, so not all are suitable for dried decorations. However, there are some glorious exceptions. Lavender retains its sculptural spiky form and deep indigo hues for several years, making it one of the most useful materials for any dried arrangement. Hops and bay leaves also dry well, as do pink-tinged marjoram and soft grey oregano. Always make sure you have plenty of material for dried arrangements – if it is used sparsely the finished effect tends to look dead, so rather than being over-ambitious about how far you think the dried herbs can stretch, it is better to scale down a design to ensure a successful end result.

CHAMOMILE FRUIT BOWL

❖

What could be more charming than to serve strawberries – or any other fresh fruit dessert – in a romantic herbal dish. Here, enchanting daisy-like chamomile flowers have been set in an aromatic base of rosemary and oregano to make a garland around a bowl. Once it is finished and filled with fruit, the bowl is concealed and the fruit is simply surrounded by an arrangement reminiscent of a summer meadow.

1 Soak the florist's foam ring in water and place on the work surface with the bowl in the centre.

2 Push in stems of oregano around the edge and top of the foam ring to make a base.

MATERIALS

FLORIST'S FOAM RING, 20 CM/8 IN INTERNAL DIAMETER

BOWL OR PLATE TO FIT INSIDE THE RING

LARGE BUNCH OREGANO

2 LARGE BUNCHES ROSEMARY

LARGE BUNCH CHAMOMILE FLOWERS

LEFT *Spare chamomile flowers placed in a glass of water make a delightful table arrangement.*

OPPOSITE *Remember to keep the foam ring well-watered to prolong the life of the display.*

3 Fill out the rest of the ring with rosemary, making sure no florist's foam shows, and that the plastic holder underneath is hidden. Finally, add the chamomile flowers.

SAGE AND MINI VEGETABLE WREATH

❖

The glorious soft grey-green tones and generous proportions of sage make it a highly effective herb for floral decorations. This wreath, decorated with miniature turnips and carrots, has a fresh, unfussy charm.

MATERIALS

SPRIGS OF SAGE (ABOUT 400 LEAVES)

MEDIUM-GAUGE FLORIST'S REEL WIRE

SECATEURS

20 MINIATURE CARROTS

10 MINIATURE TURNIPS

GREEN RAFFIA

WILLOW WREATH BASE, 40 CM/16 IN DIAMETER

ABOVE *Miniature vegetables, tied into bunches using green raffia, make a charming decorative detail.*

1 Bind the sage leaves into small bunches using the florist's wire. Put the bunches into water as you make them.

3 Wire the sage bunches on to the wreath base. Since sage wilts fairly readily, do this at the last minute. Alternatively, wire all the sage on to the wreath, then lay it in a basin of water until it is time to put it on display.

2 Tie the vegetables into bunches of two or three using green raffia.

4 Wind wire around the bunches of mini vegetables and use this to fix them to the wreath.

OPPOSITE *Hang on a kitchen wall or in the conservatory for a summer party.*

TRAPPED BAY LEAF EMBROIDERY

❖

Elegant bay leaves, overlaid with transparent tulle and stitched in place with fine running stitches, lend a quilt-like quality to this natural montage displayed in a wooden frame. You can also experiment using other dried herb leaves or dried rose petals for a different effect.

MATERIALS

PICTURE FRAME

SMALL PIECE OF NATURAL LINEN

SCISSORS

SMALL PIECE OF TULLE

6 DRIED BAY LEAVES

ALL-PURPOSE GLUE

DRESSMAKER'S PINS & NEEDLE

STRANDED EMBROIDERY THREAD

STICKY TAPE

ABOVE *The aromatic bay leaf,* Laurus nobilis.

1 Take the back off the picture frame. Cut a piece of linen slightly larger than the opening in the frame. Cut a piece of tulle the same size. Lay the linen on a flat surface and arrange the dried bay leaves in the centre. Put a tiny spot of glue on the back of each and reposition.

2 Pin the tulle over the bay leaves and sew running stitches all around the outside edges. Sew lines of running stitches vertically and horizontally between the leaves. Trim the tulle close to the perimeter stitching.

3 Turn the opened frame face down and place the embroidery face down on this, fixing it on each side with sticky tape. Put the frame together.

RIGHT *This pretty herb picture is simple and quick to make.*

SIMPLE HERB GARLAND

A simple decorative theme can be surprisingly effective. This pretty mantelpiece garland would be equally at home as a decoration for a summer birthday celebration or at Christmas.

MATERIALS

FLORIST'S WIRE

WIRE CUTTERS

SPRIGS BAY LEAVES

SECATEURS

SEAGRASS STRING

8 ARTICHOKES, OR 1 FOR EVERY 15 CM/6 IN OF GARLAND

SPRIGS ROSEMARY

ABOVE *Rosemary (*Rosmarinus officinalis) *leaves.*

OPPOSITE *Globe artichokes are the focus of this garland.*

1 Using wire cutters cut several 5 cm/2 in lengths from the florist's wire and use them to wire the leaf sprigs together in bunches.

2 Cut the seagrass string to the desired circumference of the garland plus an extra quarter. Tie on the artichokes at the desired intervals.

3 Wire the bunches of bay leaves to the seagrass string in between the artichokes.

4 Finish by twining lengths of rosemary around the seagrass string, fixing it in position with florist's wire if necessary.

SAGE TABLE DECORATION

The ruffled charm of this sage arrangement makes a deliciously aromatic tablecentre that can be co-ordinated with rosemary napkin ties. It can be made to any size required, as long as the florist's foam ball fits snugly into the top of the garden pot.

MATERIALS

FLORIST'S FOAM BALL, 9 CM/3 $^{1}/_{2}$ IN DIAMETER

MEDIUM-GAUGE FLORIST'S WIRE

SEVERAL LARGE BUNCHES SAGE (ABOUT

100 LEAVES)

SECATEURS

TERRACOTTA GARDEN POT, 9 CM/3 $^{1}/_{2}$ IN DIAMETER

OPPOSITE *This arrangement was made early in the summer when the sage stems were soft. If you make it later in the year, when they have become more woody, you will be able to fix them directly into the florist's foam without the need to wire them.*

1 Gather all the materials together and soak the foam ball in water.

2 Wire the sage into small bunches and trim the stems close to the wire.

3 Use the wire to fix the sage bunches into place on the foam ball.

4 When the ball is three-quarters covered, rest it in the garden pot to complete the arrangement.

HERB TUSSIE MUSSIE

Tussie mussies are herbal posies, which were carried in centuries gone by to overcome the "bad odours" that were then commonplace. Nowadays, their original function need not diminish the charm of an aromatic posy that can be given as a scented gift or used as a table-centre. The tussie mussie here is made from chive flowers, rosemary and comfrey, but the idea can be adapted so that any seasonal flowering herbs can be used (see right).

MATERIALS

5 CHIVE FLOWERS

LARGE BUNCH ROSEMARY

GREEN RAFFIA

SECATEURS

BUNCH COMFREY

1 M/3 FT GROSGRAIN RIBBON

RIGHT *These tiny herbal posies exude a marvellous mix of scents.*

OPPOSITE *The blue and purple tones of the chive and comfrey flowers are perfectly offset by the rich green rosemary leaves.*

1 Arrange the chive flowers in a bunch and make a circle of rosemary around them. Tie with raffia. Trim the stalks.

2 In the same way, add a "ring" of comfrey, tie it in place and trim the stalks.

3 Add a final circle of rosemary, fix in position with raffia and trim the stalks. Trim with a length of grosgrain ribbon.

LAVENDER OBELISK

This magnificent aromatic lavender obelisk, reminiscent of the elegant style of the seventeenth century, is surprisingly easy to make. However, if you do not have a lavender hedge to plunder, it could be a fairly costly project. You could scale it down or go ahead with this statuesque version, knowing that the cost will still be a fraction of the price of the bought version.

ABOVE *Dried poppy seedheads and rich rust-coloured ribbon perfectly complement the lavender.*

OPPOSITE *An elegant decoration for a hallway or to brighten the corner of a room.*

1 Using the knife, score a circle around the foam cone, about 7.5 cm/3 in up from the bottom, then carefully carve back the base so that it fits into the urn.

3 Using the pins, fix the wire-edged ribbon to the cone: start at the bottom and work around to the top, then work back down again to make a trellis effect. Scrunch the ribbon slightly as you go to give a fuller effect.

2 Try the cone in the urn. If it does not yet fit, carve away a little more of the foam until it does.

4 Position one poppy seedhead at the top of the cone, and the others at intervals around the cone to create a pleasing effect. Cut the lavender stalks to within 2.5 cm/1 in of the heads and start by fixing a ring of lavender all around the base of the obelisk where it meets the urn. Working in rows, gradually fill in each section within the ribbons.

MATERIALS

SHARP KNIFE

DRY FLORIST'S FOAM CONE, 50 CM/20 IN HIGH

METAL URN, 30 CM/12 IN DIAMETER

DRESSMAKER'S PINS

2M/2¼ YD WIRE-EDGED RIBBON, 5 CM/2 IN WIDE

12 DRIED POPPY SEEDHEADS

10 LARGE BUNCHES LAVENDER

5 As you reach a poppy seedhead, take it out so that you can place lavender near the hole, then replace it.

AROMATIC PICTURE FRAME

❖

Bay leaves dry well, retaining their soft green tones and spiky sculptural form. Use them to transform an ordinary picture frame inexpensively, then fill it with a favourite herb print.

MATERIALS

PICTURE FRAME

BAY LEAVES (ENOUGH TO MAKE TWO ROWS ON ALL SIDES OF THE FRAME)

GLUE GUN AND HOT WAX GLUE STICKS

1 Select bay leaves that are of a similar size, then, using the glue gun, fix them to the frame, stalk end outwards.

2 Work all the way around the frame, then make another layer just a little inside the first.

LEFT *This unusual picture frame can be part of a table decoration or hung on a wall.*

62

Dried Aromatic Wreath

An aromatic wreath is a decorative way to scent a room naturally. Here, the subdued pinks and purples of dried marjoram and lavender, matched by sympathetically tinted string, add up to a delightful tonal colour scheme.

MATERIALS

FLORIST'S WIRE

2 BUNCHES LAVENDER

BUNCH MARJORAM

WILLOW WREATH BASE, 38 CM/15 IN DIAMETER

1 SKEIN EACH OF DEEP PINK AND BLUE STRING

SCISSORS

1 Wire the lavender into small bunches. Repeat with the marjoram.

2 Make a row of marjoram bunches across the width of the wreath and tie into position using the deep pink string. Lay a row of lavender bunches just below the marjoram and tie them on with blue string. Repeat, alternating the marjoram and lavender, until the whole wreath is covered.

ABOVE *The bands of alternating herbs lend impact to this easy-to-make wreath.*

DRIED HOP CANDLE RING

❖

Hops have a delicate translucent beauty which they retain even when dried. But once dried the bines are brittle and hard to handle, so cut off the flowers to use for decorations. The subtle green tones team delightfully with the colourful beeswax, making hops a wonderful material for making candle rings.

MATERIALS

FLORIST'S DRIED FOAM BALL, 10 CM/4 IN DIAMETER

SHARP KNIFE

SAUCER

5 CM/2 IN THICK BEESWAX PILLAR CANDLE

50 HOP FLOWERS

SCISSORS

6 SPRIGS BAY LEAVES

SAFETY TIP
Do not leave the candle burning unattended, and be sure to extinguish it before it reaches the level of the hops.

OPPOSITE *This delightful candle ring would make an unusual table centrepiece.*

1 Cut the florist's foam ball in half, then cut a 2.5 cm/1 in thick slice off one side.

2 Place the foam disc in the saucer and fix the candle in the middle by gently pushing it through the centre of the foam.

3 Cut the hop flowers off the bine, leaving them in their clusters where possible. Push the stalks into the florist's foam to cover it completely.

4 Fix the sprigs of bay leaves into the florist's foam, placing them decoratively at regular intervals around the ring.

AROMATIC HERBAL GIFTS

THE SMELLE [OF MINT] REJOICETH THE HEART OF
MAN, FOR WHICH CAUSE THEY USED TO STREW IT
IN CHAMBERS AND PLACES OF RECREATION,
PLEASURE AND REPOSE, WHERE FEASTS AND
BANQUETS ARE MADE.

JOHN GERARD, THE HERBALL, 1597

The fragrance of herbs is one of their most enduring qualities, redolent of sunny summer days when the air is thick with nature's perfumes. Their scent may be sweet, like lavender, rose or honeysuckle; or aromatic, like sage, rosemary, thyme or bay. Scent has a powerful effect on us, and has played a major part in seduction down the ages. The ancient Egyptians used oils scented with herbs for baths and massage, passing on their skills to the Greeks. However, it was the Persians who first learned to distil oils from flowers, making the heady perfume called attar of roses which was brought back to Europe by the Crusaders to woo their lady-loves. It was not until the fourteenth century that an original perfume appeared in Europe, when Hungary water was formulated.

Named after Queen Isabella of Hungary, it contained rosemary and lavender oils and, according to legend, was given to her by a crippled hermit with the promise that it would preserve her beauty.

The evocative aromas of herb oils are not simply a pleasant luxury; according to the theory of aromatherapy inhaling the scent of certain herbs can have a positive effect on health and well-being. Partly for this reason, and partly to overcome unpleasant odours due to bad sanitation, sweet-smelling herbs were strewn on stone floors in medieval Europe, a custom that was continued right up until the nineteenth century in churches.

In the sixteenth century, potpourri was introduced as a natural room freshener and, by

Stuart times, all manner of herbal fragrances were used to scent every kind of household product, from furniture polish and candles to soap. The ladies of large houses would have a still room where they would make flower waters, herbal cosmetics, pomanders, potpourri and perfumed soaps, as well as medicinal preparations. Sweet bags, also made in the still room, were filled sometimes with lavender, sometimes with fragrant herbal powders, then placed in wardrobes and drawers to scent clothes and linen while repelling insects. Sweet bags had their heyday in Victorian times, when young girls would stitch them each year at harvest time. Even today, we use many aromatic herbal products in the form of scented soaps, herbal cosmetics and sweetly scented potpourris.

LEFT *Lavender is traditionally linked with the laundering of linens. Freshen the linen cupboard by hanging up a sprig of dried lavender or slipping lavender sachets between the sheets and tablelinens.*

RIGHT *Herbal soaps, prettily tied around with gauzy ribbon, are instantly transformed into a perfect gift.*

OPPOSITE *Flower waters were extremely popular in Victorian times, but even today they are wonderfully refreshing on hot summer days and make perfect pick-me-ups when travelling by air.*

HERBAL BATH OILS AND FLOWER WATERS

The sensual pleasure of relaxing in a warm bath perfumed with aromatic herbal oils is one that was taken to its zenith by the Romans. They turned bathing in public baths into something of a ceremony, starting by being anointed with aromatic oils in the unctuarium, followed by a cold bath in the frigidarium, a tepid one in a tepidarium and a hot one in the caldarium. Over the centuries, bathing became less popular in Europe, partly due to Christian taboo, but in eighteenth-century France, certainly amongst the nobility, bathing once again became a social pastime. It was even customary to receive guests while lounging in a scented bath, a large part of which was discreetly covered over to protect the bather's modesty.

Judging by the range of bath products available nowadays, a perfumed soak has lost none of its allure since then, though we may prefer to indulge ourselves in more privacy. As well as offering a delicious aroma, herbal baths have a therapeutic effect. You can either use the herbs themselves for a refreshing bath with a subtle

ABOVE *Prettify a bottle of bath oil by adding a bunch of herbs. Make sure the herbs are absolutely dry, then tie in bunches and push into the jar.*

OPPOSITE *Preserve the perfume of garden roses by using them to make flower waters.*

BELOW *Chamomile flowers look particularly pretty in light-coloured oils.*

scent, or you can use essential oils, which have a more concentrated perfume as well as a more marked therapeutic effect. To use the herbs directly, you will need to make a simple drawstring muslin bag. Hang the strings on the hot tap so the water can flow through the herbs, extracting their perfume. For an oil bath, run the bath first, then shake in about 10 drops of oil. Another idea is to add drops of essential oils to your favourite bath oil and shake it to mix.

Floral waters are another herbal toiletry with centuries of history. Some say lavender water was the first, crediting it to Hildegard of Bingen, a Benedictine abbess who lived in the Rhinelands during the twelfth century. In later centuries, flower waters have more generally been used as perfumed fresheners and skin toners, for men and women. Napoleon is reputed to have got through several bottles of eau-de-cologne a day! Victorian ladies used flower waters as a pick-me-up on hot summer's days.

Floral waters can be made using flowers or essential oils. In summer, before the roses and lavender are over, it is lovely to preserve their scent in some refreshing cologne. Put 1 cup of lavender flowers or rose petals into a large screw-top jar and pour over 50ml/3$^{1}/_{2}$ tbsp/ $^{1}/_{4}$ cup of vodka. Shake well and store in a dark room for six days, shaking the mixture well each day. Strain and pour into a pretty perfume bottle for use. Use within one month of making.

HERB POTPOURRI

The natural perfumes of herbs and flowers are far superior to any that are manufactured, and home-made potpourri is the perfect solution for subtle room scenting. Potpourri – the phrase comes from the French and means "rotten pot" – became widely popular in the sixteenth century, when spices and other raw materials became more widely available.

In those days, they used the moist method of making potpourri, fermenting scented petals in a pot with alternating layers of salt as a preservative. This was left to mature until it became cake-like so that it could be broken up and more perfumes and fixatives added. The resulting mixture smelled rich and exotic, though was not attractive to look at, so it was traditionally kept in elaborate china jars with perforated lids. This time-consuming and unattractive method has been superseded in recent times by dry potpourri, which is much prettier and easier to make. It consists of dried leaves, flowers and essential oils for perfume plus a fixative – very often powdered orris root, which is easily available and pleasant to handle.

It is a delightful summer occupation to make large batches of potpourri, which you can then package in clear cellophane to take as gifts when visiting friends.

SUMMER POTPOURRI

Capture the essence of summer with this wonderful sweet-scented potpourri mix.

MATERIALS

2 ML/40 DROPS LAVENDER OIL

4 ML/80 DROPS GERANIUM OIL

2 ML/40 DROPS BERGAMOT OIL

SMALL SCREW-TOP GLASS BOTTLE

25 G/1 OZ POWDERED ORRIS ROOT

SMALL BOWL

50 G/2 OZ DRIED LEMON VERBENA

175 G/6 OZ DRIED LAVENDER

225 G/8 OZ DRIED ROSEBUDS

LARGE BOWL

WOODEN SPOON

GLASS OR CHINA JAR

1 Measure out the essential oils into a small glass bottle, screw on the top and shake well. Put the orris root into a bowl and add the mixed oils drop by drop, stirring constantly to blend well. Mix the dried herbs and flowers in a large bowl and sprinkle the oil mixture on to this. Mix well using a wooden spoon. Tip the potpourri into a glass or china jar, cover, seal well and place in a warm dark place for 2-6 weeks to mature.

LEFT *Pack the potpourri mixture into cones of cellophane and tie them with toning grosgrain ribbon to make attractive gifts.*

OPPOSITE *Rose petals, lemon verbena and lavender all look decorative stored in glass jars until you are ready to make the potpourri. Here, the powdered orris root has already been measured out and placed in a small glass at the back.*

HOME-MADE HERBAL WASH BALLS

❖

Soap balls, perfumed with lavender oil, make delightful gifts when gathered up into pouches.

MATERIALS

LARGE BAR OF UNSCENTED SOAP

GRATER

MEASURING JUG

SPOON

DOUBLE SAUCEPAN

PESTLE AND MORTAR

LAVENDER ESSENTIAL OIL

ORGANZA, 30 CM/12 IN SQUARE

SCISSORS

TAFFETA RIBBON

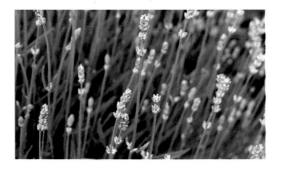

ABOVE *Lavender (*Lavandula angustifolia*)*.

OPPOSITE *Metal-shot organza makes festive packaging.*

1 Finely grate the soap using an ordinary kitchen grater. Measure out the right quantity of water – you will need one part water to two parts soap.

2 Tip the water and the soap into a double saucepan and gently heat, stirring constantly, until you have a thick paste.

3 Turn the mixture into the mortar and add 12 drops of lavender oil to each 150 g/5 oz of the original soap. Pound with the pestle and mix well to combine the ingredients thoroughly.

4 Wet your hands, take a small amount of the mixture and roll it into a ball. Repeat for each ball and leave to set hard. To package the balls once fully dry, cut a square of organza, put some wash balls in the centre, then gather up the sides to form a pouch. Secure with a taffeta ribbon.

LAVENDER MOISTURIZER

Treat yourself to some pure, home-made cosmetics. Lavender is the perfect essential oil to use in face cream as it not only smells wonderful but also helps to heal skin blemishes. Make several small batches at a time and pour it into pretty jars to make gifts for your friends – but warn them that this moisturizer is preservative-free and needs to be kept in the refrigerator.

1 Measure out the cocoa butter, borax, almond oil, lavender water and beeswax granules to the amounts required.

MATERIALS

20 G/³/₄ OZ COCOA BUTTER

10 ML/2 TSP BORAX

75 ML/5 TBSP ALMOND OIL

175 ML/6 FL OZ/³/₄ CUP LAVENDER WATER

20 ML/4 TSP BEESWAX GRANULES

MIXING BOWL

SAUCEPAN

WOODEN SPOON

SMALL PAN

8 DROPS LAVENDER ESSENTIAL OIL

GLASS JARS

2 Put the beeswax, cocoa butter and almond oil in a bowl set over a saucepan of simmering water and melt, stirring constantly. In a separate pan dissolve the borax in the lavender water by gently warming it. Add the lavender water and borax to the mixture in the bowl, stirring constantly.

3 When the cream is thoroughly combined, take it off the heat to cool. While it is still tepid, add the lavender oil and mix well.

4 Pour the moisturizer into pretty glass jars and store in the refrigerator for up to three weeks.

OPPOSITE *As the cream does not keep for very long, make up small quantities at a time.*

POTPOURRI POUCH

❖

Potpourri in bowls has a habit of getting dusty, so run up some simple bags in brightly coloured fabric and fill them with potpourri to scent your home. If you wish, you could make them in fabric offcuts to match your furnishings.

MATERIALS

2 PIECES CONTRASTING FABRIC, 15 X 40 CM/6 X 16 IN

MAIN FABRIC, 60 X 40 CM/24 X 16 IN

NEEDLE & SCISSORS

MATCHING SEWING THREAD

DRESSMAKER'S PINS

SEWING MACHINE

POTPOURRI

2 M/2$^{1}/_{4}$ YD WIRE-EDGED RIBBON,
1 CM/$^{1}/_{2}$ IN WIDE

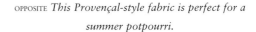

OPPOSITE *This Provençal-style fabric is perfect for a summer potpourri.*

1 Fold over and stitch a double hem along one long edge of each of the pieces of contrasting fabric. Pin the unhemmed edges, right sides together, to either end of the main fabric. Stitch.

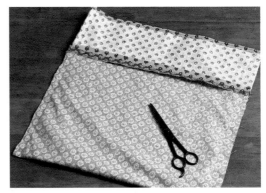

2 Press the seams open and fold the whole piece in half. Stitch the side seams.

4 Fill the bag with plenty of your favourite potpourri, shaking it down to the bottom.

5 Fold the ribbon in half, wrap it around the neck of the bag, and tie a bow. Adjust the loops and trim the ends.

3 Turn the bag to the right side and fold the contrasting facings down inside the bag.

BAY LEAF CANDLES

Nature supplies some of the prettiest ways to decorate candles. Here, deliciously aromatic bay leaves provide the perfect embellishment for simple church pillar candles. Their soft green colour contrasts beautifully with the creamy yellow of the candles.

ABOVE *Green raffia perfectly complements the soft tones of the bay leaves.*

OPPOSITE *This display would make a lovely Christmas table or mantelpiece decoration.*

1 Place a small blob of glue on the back of each leaf and fix in place around the candles.

MATERIALS

GLUE GUN AND HOT WAX GLUE STICKS

ABOUT 8 BAY LEAVES FOR EACH CANDLE

ASSORTED CHURCH PILLAR CANDLES

GREEN RAFFIA

SCISSORS

TIN BOWL

SAFETY TIP

Do not leave the candle burning unattended, and extinguish it before it reaches the bay leaves.

2 Fix securely and decoratively with green raffia, using a reef knot.

3 Trim the ends of the raffia. Stand a group of candles of various sizes in a tin bowl, securing them by dripping some hot wax into the bowl to fix the candles firmly in place.

ROSEBUD HEART

A sweetly scented rosebud heart makes an enchanting bedroom decoration or a decorative wardrobe scenter. Hang it on the inside of the wardrobe door where it will not be crushed. This simple but effective idea can be adapted to make other pretty shapes.

MATERIALS

60 CM/24 IN GARDEN WIRE

2 M/2$^1/_4$ YD PURPLE RIBBON ABOUT 1 CM/$^1/_2$ IN WIDE

GLUE GUN AND HOT WAX GLUE STICKS

25 DRIED ROSEBUDS

1 Make a hook in each end of the length of garden wire. Bend it into a heart shape and join it at the bottom by linking the hooks.

2 Starting at the middle point, bind the heart with the ribbon.

3 When you get back to the beginning, make a loop for hanging and secure it with a spot of glue.

4 Using the glue gun, fix the rosebuds to the heart shape.

OPPOSITE *This heart-shaped hanger could also be used as a romantic gift for Valentine's Day.*

AROMATIC HOT MAT

Stitch a robust ticking sachet, then fill it with aromatic herbs to make a tough mat on which to stand hot pots. As you put a pan down on it, the heat will release the herbs' rich fragrance.

MATERIALS

50 CM/ 20 IN TICKING

SCISSORS

NEEDLE

MATCHING SEWING THREAD

DRESSMAKER'S PINS

AROMATIC HERBS TO FILL: E.G. BAY LEAVES, CINNAMON, CLOVES

UPHOLSTERY NEEDLE

COTTON STRING

1 Make the hanger by cutting a strip of ticking 5 x 30 cm/2 x 12 in. Fold it in half lengthways, right sides together, and stitch along the long side. Trim the seam, turn to the right side and press. Fold in half to form a loop.

2 Cut two pieces of ticking 64 x 50 cm/25 x 20 in. Place the pieces right sides together and slip the hanger between the layers with the raw edges pointing outwards towards the corner.

4 Fill the cushion with the bay, cinnamon and cloves. Slip-stitch the opening.

OPPOSITE *Filled with bay leaves, cinnamon and cloves, this hot mat will bring wonderful aromas to your kitchen.*

5 Using a heavy duty upholstery needle threaded with cotton string, make a stitch about a third of the way in from two adjacent sides of the cushion, clearing the contents away from the area as you go. Make a simple knot to secure the tie. Untwist the strands of the string for a feathery look. Repeat with the other three ties.

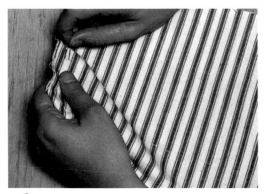

3 Pin and stitch the pieces together, leaving a small opening. Trim the seams and turn to the right side.

RIBBONED LAVENDER HEARTS

Exquisitely elegant, these linen hearts, trimmed with taffeta ribbon, are a smart way to make your wardrobe smell delicious. Made as a pair, they are designed to twist around the hanger holding a favourite garment.

MATERIALS

PAPER

PENCIL

SCISSORS

50 CM/20 IN PURPLE LINEN

1.5 M/1 1/2 YD RAYON RIBBON

DRESSMAKER'S PINS

TACKING THREAD

NEEDLE

SEWING MACHINE

MATCHING SEWING THREAD

150 G/5 OZ DRIED LAVENDER

1.5 M/1 1/2 YD TAFFETA RIBBON, 6 CM/2 1/4 IN WIDE

OPPOSITE *Too good to hide, these lavender hearts could also be used as pretty room scenters.*

1 Make a heart-shaped paper pattern 18 cm/7 in high and use it to cut out four hearts in purple linen. Fold the rayon ribbon in half lengthways and pin it, folded side in, to a heart, positioning it just inside the edge.

2 Place another linen heart shape right side down on top of the heart with the ribbon. Tack. Stitch around the edges, catching the edges of the ribbon and leaving a small opening.

3 Snip the bottom point off the heart inside the seam and clip the seam allowance around the curves. Turn to the right side and fill with lavender. Stitch to close the opening. Repeat to make a second heart.

4 Cut two 60 cm/24 in lengths from the taffeta ribbon and tie these into bows. Trim the ends. Sew one bow on to each heart. Use the remaining ribbon to link them for hanging, firmly stitching each end to the back of one heart.

GAUZY SLEEP CUSHION

Hops make an excellent filling for a cushion for the bed. Traditionally known to be mildly sedative and sleep inducing, they are also delightfully pretty. Let them become part of the design by using a translucent fabric for the top of the cushion. Lavender has been added to the filling as it induces a sense of well-being and sweetens the smell. The hops are surprisingly robust, and will keep their shape if the cushion is used decoratively on top of the sleeping pillow, rather than as a pillow itself.

ABOVE *If you cannot find hops, substitute lavender, which will make an equally attractive filling.*

OPPOSITE *Hops are too pretty to hide. Let them contribute to the design of this scented cushion by using a translucent fabric for the cover.*

MATERIALS

NATURAL LINEN, 30 CM/12 IN SQUARE

SEWING MACHINE

MATCHING SEWING THREAD

FINE MUSLIN OR OTHER TRANSLUCENT FABRIC, 30 CM/12 IN SQUARE

TACKING THREAD

NEEDLE

SCISSORS

TAPE MEASURE

DRESSMAKER'S PINS

4 HANDFULS DRIED HOP FLOWERS

2 HANDFULS DRIED LAVENDER

1.5 M/1$^{1}/_{2}$ YD WHITE RAYON RIBBON, 1 CM/$^{1}/_{2}$ IN WIDE

1 Turn in and stitch a single hem all around the linen square. Tack the muslin on top of this and trim it to the edge of the hem on the linen square. Turn the linen hem over the muslin and stitch through all layers, leaving a gap on one side.

2 Measure 6 cm/2$^{1}/_{4}$ in in from the edge of the cushion and mark with pins. Stitch along this line, removing the pins as you go, leaving half of one side open. Fill with hops and lavender and stitch across the opening.

3 Fold the rayon ribbon in half lengthways and tack over the top of the inner line of stitching on the front of the cushion. Slip-stitch the inner side of the ribbon to the cushion, and then the outer side to make a border around the visible hops.

APPLIQUÉD SACHETS

❖

It is lovely to have enough lavender sachets to scent all your drawers, and, if you keep the design simple, it will not take long to make a whole batch. You can make them up from different fabric scraps or, as here, use the same fabric but create interest by reversing it or cutting it on the cross for the appliquéd decoration.

OPPOSITE *At the end of summer, traditionally, young girls would make a whole batch of lavender sachets to give as gifts.*

1 Using blanket stitch and stranded embroidery thread, sew the heart on to the front of one of the two pieces of fabric. To work blanket stitch, bring the needle up close to the edge of the heart, then insert it again near to where you first brought it up. Bring the needle up under the edge of the heart so that it lies on top of the loop of thread and pull through. Repeat all along the edge of the heart to secure it to the square fabric.

MATERIALS

(FOR EACH SACHET)

A HEART SHAPE CUT FROM THE SACHET FABRIC, 5 CM/2 IN HIGH

2 PIECES FABRIC, 10 CM/4 IN SQUARE

STRANDED EMBROIDERY THREAD

NEEDLE

COLOURED SHELL BUTTON

DRESSMAKER'S PINS

SEWING MACHINE

MATCHING SEWING THREAD

SCISSORS

DRIED LAVENDER

50 CM/20 IN GROSGRAIN RIBBON, 1 CM/$^{1}/_{2}$ IN WIDE

2 Stitch a contrasting button just below the dip in the top of the heart. To make up the sachet, pin another square of fabric face down on the appliquéd square.

3 Stitch the two squares together, leaving a small opening. Snip off the corners and turn to the right side. Fill with lavender and slip-stitch the opening near one corner.

4 Fold the grosgrain ribbon over the edges of the lavender sachet and slip-stitch in position first on one side and then on the other.

DELICIOUS HERBS

CORIANDDRE LAYD TO WYTH BREAD OR BARLY
MELE IS GOOD FOR SAYNT ANTONYES FYRE.

WILLIAM TURNER, 1551

Adish without herbs is like a summer's day without sunshine. The ingredients are there, but the flavour lacks piquancy. Nowadays, this hardly needs saying, as many recipes include herbs, and alongside the huge array of dried herbs in the supermarkets there is an increasing choice of fresh ones too. Nothing matches the flavours of fresh herbs. Use them generously, both to improve the flavour of your cooking and because picking the leaves encourages the plant to put on more growth. If you want to retain the flavour in the leaves of your own herbs, you should never allow a plant to flower: once it is pollinated, it will no longer need to attract insects, and will put all its energy into producing seed.

The range of herbs generally used in modern cookery is fairly limited; in Tudor times they were much more adventurous. A herb garden commonly contained up to 70 types, and cooks happily used more fragrant varieties, such as lavender, in both sweet and savoury dishes. But in the Puritan age, elaborate dishes with "unnecessary" flavourings were seen as extravagant. British cuisine became even more impoverished with the onset of the Industrial Revolution, as

ABOVE *Harvest the herbs in the morning, then tie them into faggots for later use. These can be hung up to dry so their flavour can be preserved and used in cooking for months to come.*

OPPOSITE *Use generous amounts of herbs fresh from the garden.*

BELOW *Make up little muslin pouches of bouquet garni, perfect for flavouring stews and soups.*

the great migration from the country to the cities meant that fewer people had smallholdings, and the arts of growing and using culinary herbs were all but lost. It is only in recent decades, with the increase in international travel, that cooks have rekindled the use of herbs in their cooking. Skills borrowed from Italy (dating back to ancient Rome), France, the Middle East and Asia have resulted in a rich cuisine.

In America, the multi-cultural mix has led to a hugely varied cuisine, since the use of herbs was brought with settlers from their mother countries. The Shakers, a devout religious group, for instance, were enthusiastic herb growers. They harvested herbs on their farms each year, selling some and making the rest into medicines for their own use. They became well known for the quality of their herbs, which they packaged not only for the home market, but even to export back to Europe.

The delicious, fragrant flavour of herbs is a joy to share, so this chapter consists mainly of recipes for culinary herbal gifts such as oils, jellies and drinks. There are also some mouthwatering desserts which are a delight to share with friends and loved ones.

HERBAL OILS AND VINEGARS

Capture the very essence of herbs in oils and vinegars, which you can then use as ingredients in your cooking. These are a treat, so use a fine virgin olive oil, which can be used as an ingredient as well as for frying. Decant the flavoured oils and vinegars into attractive bottles and make smart wax paper tops tied around with a neat binding of cotton string.

MAKING HERB OILS AND VINEGARS

❖

Herbs for oils and vinegars should be collected in the morning after the dew has dried, but before the flavours have dissipated in the hot sun. Allow the moisture to dry completely before use, otherwise they may become mouldy. Pour the oil or vinegar into a wide-topped jar and add a large handful of herbs. Allow to steep for two weeks, then strain and decant into a pretty bottle. Add a few sprigs of fresh herbs (again making sure they are free from moisture), to indicate the flavour of the oil or vinegar.

ABOVE *Finish off the bottles by neatly winding cotton string around a wax paper top and tying it securely with a reef knot.*

OPPOSITE *Beautiful and delicious, herbal oils make exquisite gifts. From left to right: basil and chilli, Mediterranean herbs, dill and lemon, thyme and mixed herb.*

ROSEMARY AND RED WINE VINEGAR

Steep rosemary in red wine vinegar according to the instructions left, then decant and add a few long stems of rosemary plus some pink rose petals.

MIXED HERB VINEGAR

Steep sage, thyme, bay and marjoram in white wine vinegar according to the instructions left, then decant. Tie a selection of the herbs into a bunch and wind around with string. Insert into the bottle.

TARRAGON VINEGAR

Steep tarragon in cider vinegar according to the instructions left, then decant. Insert two or three long sprigs of tarragon into the bottle.

MIXED HERB OIL

Steep sage, rosemary, tarragon and marjoram in virgin olive oil according to the instructions left, then decant. Bind a selection of the herbs with string and add to the bottle. Use to pan-fry chicken or make into herby salad dressings.

DILL AND LEMON OIL

Steep a handful of fresh dill and a large strip of lemon rind in virgin olive oil according to the instructions left, then decant. Add two large fronds of dill and two strips of lemon peel to the bottle. Use to pan-fry or grill fish.

THYME OIL

Steep a handful of thyme in virgin olive oil according to the instructions left, then decant. Add two large sprigs of thyme to the bottle for decoration. Excellent for brushing over chicken before roasting.

MEDITERRANEAN HERB OIL

Steep rosemary, thyme and marjoram in virgin olive oil according to the instructions left, then decant. Decorate with herbs tied around a cinnamon stick. Add to garlicky tomato sauces, coq au vin or lamb daubes.

BASIL AND CHILLI OIL

Steep basil and three chillies in virgin olive oil according to the instructions left, then decant. Put two sprigs of basil and three chillies in the bottle to decorate. Add to tomato and mozzarella salads. This oil is particularly delicious brushed over Italian-style breads.

FRAGRANT HERBAL DRINKS

❖

Refreshing cool drinks on a hot summer's day are all the more exotic for the secret ingredient of herbs. Whether you choose soft or alcoholic drinks, add a pretty touch by freezing flowers in the ice cubes. For a summer party, serve refreshing lemonade and delicious Pimm's.

OPPOSITE *From left to right: floral ice cubes, Pimm's and fresh lemonade.*

FRESH LEMONADE

Nothing matches home-made lemonade. Slightly sharp, it makes a most refreshing drink for both children and adults.

MAKES ABOUT 24 GLASSES

2¹/₂ LEMONS, THINLY SLICED

675 G/1¹/₂ LB/3¹/₂ CUPS GRANULATED SUGAR

1.2 LITRES/2 PINTS/5 CUPS WATER

25 G/1 OZ/¹/₄ CUP CITRIC ACID

25 G/1 OZ/¹/₂ CUP LEMON BALM

To serve

ICE

CHILLED STILL OR SPARKLING MINERAL WATER

1 Put the sliced lemons in a large saucepan or preserving pan with the sugar and water. Slowly bring to the boil, stirring occasionally until the sugar has dissolved. Boil for 15 minutes then remove from the heat and stir in the citric acid. Add the lemon balm and leave to cool. Discard the lemon balm and pour the lemonade into medium-sized wide-necked bottles. Seal and chill for up to two weeks.

2 To serve, pour the lemonade into a large jug until one-third full. Add ice and top with water.

PIMM'S

A picturesque and most refreshing drink, to be served long, cool and garnished with pretty blue borage flowers on hot summer days.

1 One-third fill a large jug or tall glasses with Pimm's No 1. Add ice cubes and top up with chilled fizzy lemonade or tonic water. Decorate with thinly sliced cucumber, halved orange slices, borage flowers and mint or borage leaves.

STRAWBERRY AND LAVENDER GIN

The delicately perfumed quality of this drink makes it simply irresistible. It is perfect for summer celebrations in the garden – christenings, weddings and anniversaries.

MAKES 1 BOTTLE

400 G/14 OZ STRAWBERRIES, HULLED, THICKLY SLICED

175 G/6 OZ/1 CUP CASTER SUGAR

8 LARGE LAVENDER FLOWERS

750 ML/1¹/₄ PINTS/3 CUPS GIN

1 Put the strawberries, sugar and lavender into a large wide-necked jar. Pour on the gin and seal. Leave the jar in a cool place for seven days, giving it a gentle shake each day.

2 Strain the gin off the fruit and lavender, then pour it back into the original bottle, or into two smaller more decorative bottles. Seal well. Store in a cool place for up to four months.

HERBAL ICE BOWL

❖

Serve no-fuss desserts in an enchanting herbal ice bowl. Incredibly pretty on the table, it is also unbelievably easy to make.

RIGHT *This pretty herbal ice bowl is a very simple, but highly effective, way of impressing dinner guests.*

1 First find two bowls, either glass or plastic, that will fit one inside the other leaving a gap of about 2 cm/³/₄ in between them. Tape the bowls together across the top and put on a plate to catch any watery drips. Pour cooled boiled water (for clearer ice) into the larger of the two bowls so that it comes almost to the top. Gather an assortment of herb leaves and flowers such as variegated mint, sweet cicely, sage, pansies, violas and chive flowers, then place them in the water to make an attractive design.

2 Freeze the bowls until solid. Peel off the tape. Half-fill a washing-up bowl with hot water, sit the frozen bowls in it and pour a little hot water into the smaller bowl. Count to 30 then remove the bowls and pour the water out of the small bowl. Push a thin pointed knife blade between the ice and the edge of the larger bowl to loosen. Turn upside down and remove the large bowl. Carefully turn up the other way and put on a plate. Loosen the smaller bowl and lift out. Return to the freezer. Fill just before serving.

CRYSTALLIZED FLOWERS

Made in minutes, these pretty decorations add a delightful touch to any light summery dessert, especially creamy fruit soufflés, rich chocolate mousses or fruit trifles. Put them on the dessert at the last minute, otherwise they will go soft.

1 Brush flowers and leaves with a little raw egg white and sprinkle with caster sugar. Leave to dry for an hour or so on a large plate or cooling rack out of direct sunlight. Use on the day of making.

RIGHT *Choose from tiny blue anchusa flowers, delicate pansies, violas, tiny herb flowers, sprigs of variegated mint and fronds of sweet cicely. Pick when dry and insect free. Avoid those that may have been sprayed with insecticide.*

DECORATING WITH FLOWERS

Give desserts the perfumed taste of lavender, just as cooks did in Elizabethan times, then decorate with the prettiest of herbs.

LAVENDER SUGAR

Flavour caster sugar with lavender to lend an exotic touch to cakes, sweets and desserts. Either sprinkle it neat on to summer fruits such as strawberries, redcurrants and raspberries, or use it instead of ordinary sugar when baking and making desserts.

1 Put 1 kg/2¹/₄ lb/5 cups caster sugar into a large glass storage jar and press four large lavender flowers deep into the sugar. Seal and store for two weeks to allow the lavender to perfume the sugar.

GARDEN FLOWER PAVLOVA

Pavlova must be one of the most wickedly delicious desserts, made up of rich sticky meringue and a generous layer of whipped cream that is freshened up with seasonal fruit. Give it a perfumed flavour by using lavender sugar, then decorate it with crystallized herbs to make an enchanting dessert.

SERVES 8

For the pavlova

5 LARGE EGG WHITES

250 G/9 OZ/1¹/₄ CUPS LAVENDER SUGAR

1 TSP CORNFLOUR

5 ML/1 TSP WHITE WINE VINEGAR

To fill

300 ML/¹/₂ PINT/1¹/₄ CUPS DOUBLE CREAM

2 RIPE PEACHES

To decorate

SELECTION OF CRYSTALLIZED FLOWERS
(SEE PREVIOUS PAGE)

1 Preheat the oven to 110°C/225°F/Gas ¹/₄. Line two baking sheets with baking parchment and draw a 23 cm/9 in circle on one and a 16 cm/6¹/₂ in circle on the second piece (or use dinner plates as guides).

2 Put the egg whites in a large bowl and whisk until they form stiff but moist-looking peaks. Gradually whisk in the sugar a spoonful at a time and continue whisking for two minutes until the meringue is thick and glossy.

3 Mix the cornflour and vinegar together and fold into the meringue mixture. Using two dessertspoons, drop spoonfuls of meringue over the smaller circle. Make the larger circle in the same way, and level the centre slightly. Cook for 1¹/₄ hours or until pale golden. (Swap the positions of the baking sheets during cooking so that the layers cook to an even colour.) The meringues should come away from the paper easily: test by peeling away an edge of the paper, then leave to cool still on the paper.

4 To serve, remove the paper and put the larger meringue on a large flat serving plate. Softly whip the cream and spoon over the meringue. Halve, stone and slice the peaches and arrange on the cream. Place the second meringue on top of the peaches. Chill. When ready to serve, decorate with crystallized flowers and serve immediately.

OPPOSITE *Add the flowers just before serving. They will go soft if placed on a finished pavlova which is still being kept in the refrigerator.*

WARM HERBY BREAD

This mouth-watering Italian-style bread, flavoured with basil, rosemary, olive oil and sun-dried tomatoes, is absolutely delicious served warm with fresh salads and sliced salami or Parma ham. The olive oil not only lends a delicious flavour to the bread, but also helps it to keep longer, so you can make it the day before eating it if necessary.

MAKES 3 LOAVES

1 TSP CASTER SUGAR

900 ML/1¹/₂ PINTS/3³/₄ CUPS WARM WATER

1 TBSP DRIED YEAST

1.5 KG/3 LB/12 CUPS STRONG PLAIN FLOUR

1 TBSP FINE SALT

5 TBSP MIXED FRESH CHOPPED BASIL AND ROSEMARY LEAVES

50 G/2 OZ/1 CUP DRAINED SUN-DRIED TOMATOES, ROUGHLY CHOPPED

150 ML/1/4 PINT/2/3 CUP VIRGIN OLIVE OIL

To finish

EXTRA VIRGIN OLIVE OIL

ROSEMARY

SEA SALT FLAKES

OPPOSITE *Baked bread, still warm from the oven, brings additional pleasures to eating al fresco.*

1 Put the sugar into a small bowl, pour on 150 ml/¹/₄ pint/²/₃ cup warm water, then sprinkle the yeast over the top. Leave in a warm place for 10-15 minutes, until frothy. Put the flour, salt, herbs and sun-dried tomatoes into a large bowl. Add the oil and frothy yeast mixture then gradually mix in the remaining warm water with a spoon.

2 As the mixture becomes stiffer, bring it together with your hands. Mix to a soft but not sticky dough, adding a little extra water if needed. Turn the dough out on to a lightly floured surface and knead for five minutes until smooth and elastic. Put the dough back into the bowl, cover loosely with oiled cling film and put in a warm place for 30-40 minutes or until doubled in size.

3 Knead again until smooth and elastic, then cut into three pieces. Shape each into an oval loaf about 18 cm/7 in long, and arrange on oiled baking sheets. Slash the top of each loaf with a knife in a criss-cross pattern. Loosely cover and leave in a warm place for 15-20 minutes until well risen. Preheat the oven to 220°C/425°F/Gas 7. Brush the loaves with a little olive oil and sprinkle with rosemary leaves and salt flakes. Cook for about 25 minutes until golden brown. The bases should sound hollow when tapped.

THYME AND MUSTARD BISCUITS

These aromatic digestive-type biscuits are delicious served with one of the herby cheeses opposite as a light savoury last course.

MAKES ABOUT 40

175 G/6 OZ/1¹/₂ CUPS WHOLEMEAL FLOUR

50 G/2 OZ/¹/₂ CUP MEDIUM OATMEAL

25 G/1 OZ/2 TBSP CASTER SUGAR

10 ML/2 TSP BAKING POWDER

30 ML/2 TBSP FRESH THYME LEAVES

SALT

FRESHLY GROUND BLACK PEPPER

50 G/2 OZ/4 TBSP BUTTER

25 G/1 OZ/2 TBSP WHITE VEGETABLE FAT

45 ML/3 TBSP MILK

10 ML/2 TSP DIJON MUSTARD

30 ML/2 TBSP SESAME SEEDS

1 Preheat the oven to 200°C/400°F/Gas 6. Put the flour, oatmeal, sugar, baking powder, thyme leaves and seasoning into a bowl and mix. Cut the fats into pieces and add to the bowl, then rub in to form fine crumbs. Mix the milk and mustard together, stir into the flour mixture and continue mixing until you have a soft but not sticky dough.

ABOVE RIGHT *Pack small piles of biscuits in cellophane and tie with string or ribbon for a savoury gift.*

2 Knead lightly on a floured surface then roll out to a thickness of 5 mm/¹/₄ in. Stamp out 5 cm/2 in rounds with a fluted biscuit cutter and arrange, spaced slightly apart, on two greased baking sheets. Reroll the trimmings and continue stamping out biscuits until all the dough is used. Prick the biscuits with a fork and sprinkle with sesame seeds. Cook for 10-12 minutes until lightly browned, alternating baking sheets on the oven shelves during cooking for an even colour. Cool on the trays then pack into a small biscuit tin. Store in a cool place for up to five days.

A Quartet of Herby Cheeses

❖

Light, fragrant and charmingly pretty, these cheeses make a perfect light lunch or elegant cheese course – or package them up in waxed parchment and take them as a gift when invited out to dinner. Choose a selection of different goats' cheeses, feta and cream cheese, or mix types depending on your own preference.

DILL AND PINK PEPPERCORN CHEESE

Unwrap a 150 g/5 oz pack of "mild" medium fat goats' cheese and put on a plate. Finely chop a few sprigs of fresh dill and mix with $^1/_2$ tsp crushed pink peppercorns. Sprinkle over the cheese and press in place with the back of a spoon until lightly coated. Wrap in squares of waxed paper or baking parchment and chill until required. Use within three days.

THYME AND CHOPPED GARLIC CHEESE

Unwrap a 100 g/3$^3/_4$ oz round of full fat goats' cheese and put on a plate. Pull the leaves off several thyme stems and break any flowers into small pieces. Finely chop a clove of garlic and press the thyme and garlic over the cheese until lightly coated. Wrap and store as left.

MINTED FETA

Cut the wrapper off a 200 g/7 oz pack of feta cheese, drain and cut into small dice. Finely chop a small bunch of fresh mint, then roll the feta in mint until lightly coated. Wrap and store as left.

TARRAGON AND LEMON CHEESE

Turn a 200 g/7 oz pack of low fat soft or cream cheese out on to a plate and cut into two squares. Tear the leaves off a small bunch of fresh tarragon, finely chop and use to coat the cheeses lightly. Sprinkle with the coarsely grated rind of $^1/_2$ lemon (alternatively, make rind curls using a lemon zester). Wrap and store as left.

ABOVE *Clockwise from left: Dill and pink peppercorn, tarragon and lemon, minted feta, and thyme and chopped garlic cheese.*

HERBAL PRESERVES

Home-made preserves, packed with flavour from the summer months, are now a rare treat. These two savoury jellies, and savoury herbal plums, will add piquancy to simple meat dishes right through the year.

MINT AND APPLE JELLY

The vibrant flavour of this fresh mint-speckled jelly makes the perfect accompaniment to a delicious dinner of roast lamb.

MAKES 4 SMALL JARS

1.5 KG/3 LB COOKING APPLES

150 ML/^{1}/$_4$ PINT/^{2}/$_3$ CUP CIDER VINEGAR

750 ML/1^1/$_4$ PINTS/3 CUPS WATER

500-675 G/1^1/$_4$-1^1/$_2$ LB/3-3^1/$_2$ CUPS GRANULATED SUGAR

4 TBSP FRESH CHOPPED MINT

FEW DROPS GREEN FOOD COLOURING (OPTIONAL)

FIG OR VINE LEAVES

GREEN TWINE

1 Roughly chop the apples, including cores and skin, and put into a preserving pan. Add the vinegar and water and bring to the boil. Reduce the heat and simmer the contents for 30 minutes or until the apples are pulpy.

2 Rinse a jelly bag with boiling water, then empty the water out. Hang it from a drawer knob or upturned stool and place a large bowl underneath. Make sure the bag is not directly in contact with the bowl. Spoon the apple mixture into the bag and leave to drip for several hours.

3 Measure the juice and pour back into the preserving pan. For every 600 ml/1 pint/2^1/$_2$ cups of juice, add 450 g/1 lb/2 cups sugar. Slowly bring to the boil, stirring occasionally, until the sugar has completely dissolved. Boil rapidly for 10-15 minutes or until setting point is reached. Skim the jelly with a perforated spoon. Stir in the chopped mint, and add a few drops of green food colouring if you wish. Ladle into warm dry jars through a jam funnel. Cover the surface of the jelly with waxed paper discs and seal with cellophane discs and elastic bands. Leave to cool. Decorate the tops with fig or vine leaves tied in place with green twine. Store in a cool place for up to six months.

APPLE, STRAWBERRY AND ROSEMARY JELLY

The fragrant combination of both sweet and savoury ingredients make this a truly versatile jelly. Serve it with whipped cream on scones, or team it with roast pork or turkey.

MAKES 5 MEDIUM-SIZED JARS

900 G/2 LB COOKING APPLES

1.2 LITRES/2 PINTS/5 CUPS WATER

900 G/2 LB STRAWBERRIES

1 KG/2^1/$_4$ LB/5 CUPS GRANULATED SUGAR

5 STEMS ROSEMARY

FIG OR VINE LEAVES

GREEN TWINE

1 Chop the apples, including cores and skin, and put in a preserving pan with the water. Bring to the boil and simmer for 15 minutes. Thickly slice the strawberries, add to the pan, bring back to the boil and simmer for 15 minutes. Strain as for Mint and Apple Jelly, left.

2 Measure the juice and add 450 g/1 lb/2 cups sugar to every 600 ml/1 pint/2^1/$_2$ cups juice. Dissolve the sugar slowly then boil rapidly until setting point is reached. Skim the jelly and ladle into jars. Cool for 10 minutes then add a sprig of rosemary to each jar. Cover with waxed paper and seal with cellophane discs and elastic bands. Leave to cool. Decorate and store as for Mint and Apple Jelly, left.

LEFT *Mint and apple jelly.*

PICKLED PLUMS DE PROVENCE

These savoury plums are truly surprising and make a tasty and unusual accompaniment to cold roast turkey, chicken or pork. Unusually for such exotic fare, they are very easy to make.

MAKES 1 MEDIUM AND 1 SMALL PRESERVING JAR

1.5 KG/3 LB FIRM, UNBRUISED PLUMS

4 SPRIGS ROSEMARY

4 SMALL BAY LEAVES

4 LAVENDER FLOWERS

2 SPRIGS THYME

4 UNPEELED GARLIC CLOVES

900 ML/1 $^1/_2$ PINTS/3$^3/_4$ CUPS WHITE
WINE VINEGAR

500 G/1 $^1/_4$ LB/2 $^1/_2$ CUPS GRANULATED SUGAR

1 Remove the rubber seals from the preserving jars and warm in the oven. Prick the plums and pack tightly into the warmed jars, tucking the herbs and garlic around them. Put the vinegar in a saucepan, add the sugar and slowly bring to the boil, stirring occasionally until the sugar has dissolved. Boil rapidly for 6-7 minutes until syrupy.

2 Pour the syrup over the plums, making sure that they are completely covered. Replace the rubber seals and close the jars tightly. Leave to cool. Store in a cool place for at least a month before using, to allow the flavours to develop.

ABOVE *From left to right: Apple, strawberry and rosemary jelly, mint and apple jelly and pickled plums de Provence.*

ROSEMARY AND RATAFIA CREAM

Turn fresh summer fruits into something very special by serving them with aromatic herb creams. They are extraordinarily easy to make and add a wonderfully exotic touch to the simplest of desserts for busy cooks.

SERVES 6

300 ML/¹/₂ PINT/1¹/₄ CUPS DOUBLE CREAM

3 X 7.5 CM/3 IN SPRIGS OF FRESH ROSEMARY

25 G/1 OZ/¹/₂ CUP RATAFIA BISCUITS

To serve

400 G/14 OZ STRAWBERRIES

200 G/7 OZ RASPBERRIES

STRAWBERRY LEAVES AND FLOWERS (OPTIONAL)

SMALL SPRIG FRESH ROSEMARY

1 Put the cream in a small saucepan and bring just to the boil. Take off the heat and add the large rosemary sprigs. Leave to cool, cover, then transfer to the fridge and chill for three hours or overnight if possible.

2 Strain the cream into a bowl and discard the rosemary. Whisk the cream until softly peaking. Crush the biscuits with your fingers then fold into the cream. Spoon into a small bowl and place in the centre of a large plate.

3 Arrange the berries around the dish of cream and decorate with strawberry leaves and flowers if available. Add a tiny sprig of rosemary to the cream. Chill until ready to serve.

LEFT *Serve the cream in a small bowl surrounded by summer fruits.*

HERBAL TEAS

As well as being very refreshing, herbal teas have therapeutic qualities. Lavender tea is thought to ease depression and migraines and aid the digestion, while lime flower tea soothes tension and aids sleep, and chamomile aids digestion. The fresh or dried herbs are infused in freshly boiled water, just as for ordinary China or Indian tea, though the flavour is a lot more subtle. You can buy herbal tea loose or in tea bags. However, it looks much prettier in its loose form, and can be transformed into lovely gifts when packaged in cellophane and accompanied by an infusing spoon so that the recipient can make individual cups whenever they wish.

ABOVE AND RIGHT *Make up a herbal tea gift by packing a basket with packets of rose and lemon verbena tea, an infuser and two toning cups. Photocopy old botanical prints for labels and colour them.*

HERB DIRECTORY

WHAT GREATER DELIGHT IS THERE THAN TO
BEHOLD THE EARTH APPARELLED WITH PLANTS,
AS WITH A ROBE OF EMBROIDERED WORKE ...
IF THIS VARIETIE AND PERFECTION OF COLOURS
MAY AFFECT THE EIE, IT IS SUCH IN HERBS
AND FLOURES.

JOHN GERARD, THE HERBALL, 1597

The herbals of old (and indeed, Mrs Grieves' *A Modern Herbal* of the twentieth century) listed hundreds of herbs with their descriptions, cultivation, properties, history and folklore. Although space does not allow this directory to even attempt to emulate them, it has been included to provide a reference to complement the rest of the book, and to outline the salient points of more than 50 of the most popular and important herbs. The herbs have been arranged in alphabetical order under their Latin names, with their common names underneath.

Where reference is made to infusions and decoctions, they are made to the strengths as outlined on page 12. Do not be tempted to make them stronger than recommended because, although they are natural remedies, herbs can have a powerful effect. As well as using this list to make your own simple remedies, it can be used as a reference when buying ready-made herbal remedies at health stores.

Achillea millefolium
YARROW

This tall, vibrant plant, with its golden plate-like flowers, grows in field, meadow and roadside. It is said to be named after Achilles, who used it to heal his warriors' wounds during the Trojan War. "Soldier's woundwort" is a country name for yarrow.

■ **CULTIVATION** Yarrow grows readily with little care. When it dies down in autumn, dig it up before the frosts, divide the roots, then replant.
■ **MEDICINAL USES** Yarrow tea, sweetened with honey or sugar, helps to relieve bad colds accompanied by a fever. Fresh yarrow, applied externally, helps to staunch the flow of blood.
■ **CULINARY USES** Finely chopped young leaves give a peppery taste to salads.

Alchemilla vulgaris
LADY'S MANTLE

An attractive plant with leaves up to 15 cm/6 in across and delicate yellow-green flowers which appear from late spring to early autumn. It grows to 45 cm/18 in. Legend has it that it was used by alchemists in attempts to make gold. It is named after the Virgin Mary.

■ **CULTIVATION** Likes a cool, damp climate. Easy to grow in nearly all soils, sun or partial shade. Propagate by seed, or by dividing in spring or autumn.
■ **MEDICINAL USES** Alchemilla tea helps to regulate excessive periods.
■ **CULINARY USES** Can be used to garnish salad.

LEFT *Herbs come in all shapes, sizes and colours.*

Allium sativum
GARLIC

The various allium species all possess the familiar sulphurous smell, but individually they are valued as vegetables, herbs, medicines and decorative garden bulbs. When grown for culinary use, garlic produces better bulbs if it is not allowed to go to seed, so the white pom-pom flowers should be removed.

■ **CULTIVATION** Garlic flourishes best in rich, limy soil, though it will thrive in most soils. Plant individual cloves in early spring in a sunny spot and lift for use when the leaves begin to wither in late summer.
■ **MEDICINAL USES** See Wild Garlic on opposite page.
■ **CULINARY USES** See Wild Garlic on opposite page.

Allium schoenoprasum

CHIVES

Allium ursinum

WILD GARLIC

Aloysia triphylla

LEMON VERBENA

Anethum graveolens

DILL

Angelica archangelica

ANGELICA

A grass-like plant that produces pink pom-pom-like flowers in early summer. Although it can be found wild in moist soils, it is usually cultivated. It is a popular decorative herb for border edging and also for attracting bees.

■ CULTIVATION Grows in almost any soil. Propagate by dividing it in spring or autumn and replanting clumps of about six little bulbs.
■ MEDICINAL USES It stimulates appetite and aids digestion. It is also high in vitamin C.
■ CULINARY USES A delicious mild onion-like flavour makes this perfect for salads and to garnish vegetables.

Wild garlic, or ramsons (*Allium ursinum*), grows abundantly in woodlands and the chopped leaves can be used in cooking to give a mild garlic flavour.

■ MEDICINAL USES Prized for at least 5,000 years, garlic has long been known to reduce blood cholesterol. It is also a powerful antiseptic: when eaten raw, garlic is said to clear the digestive tract of harmful organisms without affecting the beneficial ones. It helps to relieve respiratory infections. The raw juice is a powerful disinfectant.
■ CULINARY USES Used widely in the traditional cuisines of the Mediterranean, Asia and Africa. Usually crushed or chopped, it can also be boiled, baked or fried whole.

Strongly scented, lemon verbena was brought from South America to Europe by the Spanish in the seventeenth century. A half-hardy woody shrub with pretty elongated leaves and tiny, pale lilac to white flowers, it grows up to 1.2 m/4 ft.

■ CULTIVATION Plant in a sunny sheltered spot. In autumn, prune and cover with straw to protect from frost. New growth may not appear until well into the summer.
■ MEDICINAL USES It helps to relieve feverish colds and indigestion.
■ CULINARY USES It is delicious made into a tea. Also try using fresh young leaves to flavour summer drinks and puddings.

Growing to 75 cm/2½ ft, dill has pretty feathery leaves and delicate lacy flowers. Its name comes from the old Norse word *dilla*, which means "to lull", indicating one of its properties. It was popular amongst magicians in the Middle Ages.

■ CULTIVATION Sow seeds in spring in drills 25 cm/10 in apart, then thin out to 25 cm/10 in each way when the seedlings are large enough. Water when the soil is dry to the touch.
■ MEDICINAL USES Dill oil helps to relieve flatulence and other digestive disorders. The seeds are rich in mineral salts.
■ CULINARY USES Use fresh leaves to flavour fish dishes; whole or ground seeds for pickling cucumbers.

An elegant biennial plant that reaches up to 1.8 m/6 ft tall. Thought to be named after Archangel Michael, as it was supposed to flower on his day.

■ CULTIVATION Sow ripe seeds in late summer in a shady position where they are to grow, about 90 cm/3 ft apart. The plants may not mature the first year. Keep moist.
■ MEDICINAL USES Should not be given to diabetics. Infusions can be used to loosen phlegm, relieve bronchitis, indigestion and flatulence. Used as a poultice, it can help to relieve chest and lung infections.
■ CULINARY USES The crystallized stems make attractive decorations for cakes and puddings.

Anthriscus cerefolium
CHERVIL

An aromatic biennial, often grown as an annual. It is a pretty plant reaching 38 cm/ 15 in, with feathery foliage and delicate white flowers.

■ **CULTIVATION** Easily grown in garden soil. It is especially good in containers in cool, shady positions and combines well with other shade-loving culinary herbs such as pineapple mint and golden lemon balm.
■ **MEDICINAL USES** Infusions aid digestion.
■ **CULINARY USES** Delicious flavouring when chopped and added near the end of cooking to sauces, chicken and white fish dishes. It can also be used raw in salads or as a garnish.

Arnica montana
ARNICA

An aromatic herb with daisy-like orange-yellow flowers rising up to 60 cm/2 ft from a flat rosette of leaves.

■ **CULTIVATION** Arnica thrives in most soils. Can be propagated by root division in spring, or by seeds sown in early spring in a cold frame. Seedlings can be brought outside when the frosts are over. It is an alpine so needs a cool climate and dislikes wet winters.
■ **MEDICINAL USES** The flowers are made into a tincture to relieve bruises and sprains. It also makes a good footbath – add 15 g/$^1/_2$ oz tincture to a bowl of warm water.
■ **CULINARY USES** None – can be poisonous.

Artemisia dracunculus
FRENCH TARRAGON

Grows up to 1 m/3 ft and has long narrow leaves; rarely produces flowers. It is hardy to several degrees of frost.

■ **CULTIVATION** Propagate by dividing roots in spring. Alternatively, take cuttings from the new spring growth and keep young plants under glass until the frosts are over. Plant in a sunny position and keep quite dry. Cover with straw if hard frosts are expected. Use fresh from midsummer to early autumn. If you want to dry tarragon, cut it right down in late summer and hang up to dry.
■ **MEDICINAL USES** Tarragon is beneficial to the heart and liver.
■ **CULINARY USES** It has a faintly aniseed taste that is delicious in sauces, with chicken and in salads.

Borago officinalis
BORAGE

An annual with large hairy leaves and a profusion of star-like blue flowers that bloom at the top of the stem. Reaches 75 cm/2$^1/_2$ ft. Traditionally said to lend courage and gladness.

■ **CULTIVATION** Grows in ordinary soil from seeds sown in spring. Sow in drills 38 cm/15 in apart and thin out to 45 cm/18 in apart. Will self-seed every year.
■ **MEDICINAL USES** Stimulates the kidneys. Traditionally used in France to relieve fevers and respiratory problems.
■ **CULINARY USES** The flowers make a pretty salad garnish. Traditionally used to garnish Pimm's, an alcoholic summer drink.

Buxus sempervirens
BOX

Usually grown as a hardy evergreen hedging shrub, if left alone box would grow to 4.5 m/ 15 ft. Box is dense and leafy, with pale green, petal-less flowers appearing in spring.

■ **CULTIVATION** Needs sun or semi-shade and any soil that is not waterlogged. Promote bushy growth in spring by pruning stems back to 30 cm/12 in or less. Trim to retain shape in summer.
■ **MEDICINAL USES** Decoction can be used to relieve rheumatism and, in the past, was thought to be a remedy for syphilis. The oil has been used to relieve piles, epilepsy and toothache.
■ **CULINARY USES** None – all parts are toxic if eaten.

Cichorium intybus
CHICORY

The lower leaves of chicory are broad, similar to a miniature lettuce, and from this grows a tall stem up to 1.5 m/5 ft with smaller, hairy leaves. The flowers are clear blue. The inner leaves, called chicons, are often forced in darkness and sold for salad.

■ **CULTIVATION** A hardy perennial that will grow in any soil. Propagate by sowing seeds in spring, thinning to 25 cm/10 in apart. Water in dry weather.
■ **MEDICINAL USES** Bruised leaves made into a poultice soothe inflammation.
■ **CULINARY USES** Use chicons for salads.

Coriandrum sativum
CORIANDER

A pretty annual with broad scalloped lower leaves and finely cut filligree upper leaves. It has delicate white to mauve flowers in umbels. It was used as a love potion in the Middle Ages, which was possibly effective as in large quantities it can be mildly narcotic.

■ **CULTIVATION** Sow seeds in spring in a warm dry soil in a sunny position. Do not overwater.
■ **MEDICINAL USES** Infusions are used to aid digestion and ease colic.
■ **CULINARY USES** Coriander seeds are used in curries, chutneys and pies; leaves are used to flavour salads, stews and sauces.

Eruca vesicaria ssp. *sativa*
ROCKET

This biennial native of the Mediterranean first produces broad oval leaves, then a stem of about 1 m/3 ft with pointed leaves and small white flowers. It is a fast-growing annual which was originally a popular salad leaf in Roman times.

■ **CULTIVATION** Sow seeds from late winter to early summer in a warm sunny position and do not overwater.
■ **MEDICINAL USES** Traditionally used for scurvy, it can also be used as a tonic, a mild stimulant and as part of a cough remedy. Best taken as an infusion.
■ **CULINARY USES** The lower leaves are delicious in salads. Keep picking them to encourage more growth.

Filipendula ulmaria
MEADOWSWEET

A hardy perennial that reaches 1.2 m/4 ft. Large clusters of tiny creamy-white almond-scented flowers are borne from midsummer to early autumn with large, deep green indented leaves. A favourite strewing herb of Elizabeth I.

■ **CULTIVATION** Propagate by sowing seeds in early spring, or by division in autumn or spring. Meadowsweet likes moist conditions, so plant in semi-shade.
■ **MEDICINAL USES** Decoction of roots eases shortness of breath and wheezing. Helps to loosen phlegm. Make an infusion to use against fever. Helps relieve heartburn and indigestion.
■ **CULINARY USES** Almond-like flavouring for jams and stewed fruit.

Foeniculum vulgare
FENNEL

A tall perennial brought to Britain by the Romans. Grows to 2.1 m/7 ft, with a cloud of filligree leaves and yellow flowers in umbels. Succulent bulbous root.

■ **CULTIVATION** Propagate by sowing seeds in autumn or spring, or by division in autumn. Ensure it has a dry sunny position.
■ **MEDICINAL USES** Fennel tea aids the digestion, griping pains and flatulence.
■ **CULINARY USES** Seed is used in curries and other spicy sauces. The bulb is a delicious vegetable and can be baked with cream and cheese, or grated raw into salads.

Fragaria vesca
WILD STRAWBERRY

Galium odoratum
SWEET WOODRUFF

Geranium maculatum
CRANESBILL

Helichrysum italicum
CURRY PLANT

Hypericum perforatum
ST JOHN'S WORT

Pretty, toothed evergreen leaves make this a decorative plant for the borders as well as in the kitchen garden. Grows to 25 cm/10 in and produces much-loved red fruit. The wild fruit is a lot smaller than the cultivated, but has a more concentrated flavour.

■ **CULTIVATION** Grows easily in most soils. Runners produce new plants.
■ **MEDICINAL USES** Strawberry tea relieves diarrhoea. Juice rubbed over the face relieves sunburn.
■ **CULINARY USES** Delicious fruit eaten fresh on its own, with cream, or in puddings and ices.

Pretty, hardy perennial woodland plant with star-like whorls of leaves growing at intervals on stems up to 30 cm/12 in tall. White clusters of star-like flowers at the top of the stems. Its sweet odour when dried makes it a favourite for potpourris.

■ **CULTIVATION** Plant in moist shady conditions. Propagate by division in spring or autumn. It makes good deciduous ground cover in shady areas.
■ **MEDICINAL USES** Has a healing effect, and fresh bruised leaves may be applied to cuts and grazes.
■ **CULINARY USES** None.

This is a decorative semi-evergreen perennial growing to 60 cm/2 ft. It is a popular garden plant with scalloped leaves and attractive delicately veined flowers which are borne over a long period during the summer months. It is traditionally a popular Native American herb.

■ **CULTIVATION** Cranesbill will grow in all but waterlogged soil. They prefer sun to shade. Propagate by seeds sown in early autumn or spring.
■ **MEDICINAL USES** Drink an infusion to relieve diarrhoea and piles.
■ **CULINARY USES** None.

Pretty silver foliage and clusters of yellow flowers make this a popular border plant for knot gardens. It has aromatic grey-green foliage and papery, "everlasting" flowers. The whole plant smells strongly of curry, especially after rain. It grows to 45 cm/18 in and was originally from southern Europe. The essential oil is sometimes used in cosmetics.

■ **CULTIVATION** Likes dry, sunny positions. Propagate from semi-ripe cuttings in summer.
■ **MEDICINAL USES** None.
■ **CULINARY USES** Can be used to flavour curries and spicy dishes. Should be removed before serving.

A herbaceous perennial growing to 1 m/3 ft. A native of woods and hedgerows in Europe and temperate Asia, it has pale green leaves and yellow flowers.

■ **CULTIVATION** It is not often cultivated, but will grow readily in any soil. Propagate from seed or division in autumn or spring.
■ **MEDICINAL USES** Taken as an infusion, St John's wort relieves respiratory, digestive and urinary problems and nervous tension. It is important to avoid over-exposure to sunlight during treatment as the plant causes photosensitivity.
■ **CULINARY USES** None.

Hyssopus officinalis
HYSSOP

Juniperus communis
JUNIPER

Laurus nobilis
BAY

Lavandula angustifolia
LAVENDER

Lavandula stoechas
FRENCH LAVENDER

An attractive semi-evergreen sub-shrub that grows to about 60 cm/2 ft with narrow pointed leaves and clusters of blue, pink or white flowers on the top part of the stem. Used in biblical times to purify temples and treat leprosy.

■ CULTIVATION Plant in a warm sunny spot in light soil, and water well until established. Propagate from seed in autumn or spring, or softwood cuttings in summer.

■ MEDICINAL USES Hyssop tea made from the flowers helps to relieve colds, coughs and catarrh. The infusion can also be used externally to relieve muscular pains such as rheumatism.

■ CULINARY USES Add flowers to salads.

A shrubby conifer that reaches 2 m/6 ft, valued for its berries which produce a useful oil. They also make popular ornamental plants.

■ CULTIVATION Junipers grow in limestone areas. Propagate from seeds sown under cover in autumn or spring.

■ MEDICINAL USES An infusion of juniper can be taken as a diuretic, and to relieve indigestion, flatulence and diseases of the kidney and bladder.

■ CULINARY USES The berries, which are the principal flavouring in gin, can be added to casseroles, pies and pâtés made with pork or game.

A small evergreen tree, reaching 7 m/23 ft in northern climates, up to 18 m/60 ft in warmer climes. It has narrowly oval, dark green leaves and insignificant yellow flowers that produce black fruits. It is a popular shrub, often grown as an ornamental.

■ CULTIVATION Needs fertile, well-drained soil in a sheltered sunny position. Can be grown in a pot. Prune to shape in summer. Propagate from semi-ripe cuttings in summer.

■ MEDICINAL USES Bay tea aids digestion.

■ CULINARY USES Its delicious, aromatic flavour makes bay a favourite ingredient in soups, stews and sauces, with game or fish.

A highly aromatic evergreen plant that comes in many varieties with grey-green leaves that can be long and thin or feathery. The spike-like flowers are usually purple, but can also be white, pink or green. It is one of the most popular plants for herb gardens, having subtle colouring and a delightful fragrance. French lavender (*Lavandula stoechas*) has two large butterfly-like bracts on each spike.

■ CULTIVATION Lavender likes well-drained soil and a sunny position. Propagate from seed in autumn, or by semi-ripe cutting in summer. Do not over-water. Prune back a little in spring to encourage bushiness.

■ MEDICINAL USES Lavender oil can be used neat to aid the rapid healing of burns, acne and other skin problems. It relieves headaches when a drop is placed on each temple. Lavender tea can aid digestion. The aroma of lavender (fresh or dried) can calm an irritable child and promote a sense of well-being.

■ CULINARY USES Lavender can be used instead of rosemary in lamb and fish dishes. Adds an aromatic flavour to sugar and jams.

Levisticum officinale
LOVAGE

Lonicera
HONEYSUCKLE

Melissa officinalis
LEMON BALM

Mentha spicata
SPEARMINT

Mentha x piperita
PEPPERMINT

A striking hardy perennial, lovage has large glossy leaves and reaches a height of 2.1 m/ 7 ft. It is an extremely useful herb in that it produces new shoots in early spring when few other herbs are available. Clusters of yellow flowers appear in summer, followed by tiny, aromatic seeds.

■ **CULTIVATION** Planted in rich, moist, well-drained soil, lovage needs very little attention, and will come up year after year.
■ **MEDICINAL USES** Infusions can be drunk to relieve rheumatism. This must never be drunk during pregnancy.
■ **CULINARY USES** Add leaves to soups and stews; the stems can be candied like angelica.

A group of 100 or more pretty evergreen or semi-evergreen climbing shrubs with long trumpet-like flowers. Although most honeysuckles are grown for their scent and their flowers, at least a dozen can be used medicinally, including *Lonicera japonica* (Japanese honeysuckle).

■ **CULTIVATION** Plant in well-drained fertile soil. Propagate from seed in autumn or spring, or from semi-ripe cuttings in summer. Prune only to remove dead flowers and dead wood.
■ **MEDICINAL USES** Drink honeysuckle tea to relieve chesty coughs and 'flu symptoms.
■ **CULINARY USES** None.

A lemon-scented perennial that reaches 1 m/3 ft. It has oval, toothed green leaves and inconspicuous yellow flowers. It has been cultivated for over 2,000 years and was originally grown as a bee plant. Perhaps this is why it is traditionally thought to contain the "elixir of life".

■ **CULTIVATION** Lemon balm thrives in full sun. Keep moist.
■ **MEDICINAL USES** An infusion helps to relieve depression, bronchial catarrh and colds.
■ **CULINARY USES** Lemon balm is delicious in white sauces, for fish, poultry or pork. It is also a good flavouring for summer drinks, including water.

One of a large group of perennial plants including peppermint, spearmint and pennyroyal, all of which hybridize readily. They are generally upright and leafy, reaching a height of 1 m/3 ft. Herbalists have praised the distinctive fresh smell of mint since ancient times. It is menthol which gives all mint its distinctive smell and taste. Menthol is cooling to the tongue and is also a mild anaesthetic. Spearmint is one of the world's most popular flavours and is grown commercially in Europe, USA and Asia. Mints are extremely easy to grow and most flower from summer to early autumn.

■ **CULTIVATION** Mint prefers cool damp situations, but will grow and spread almost anywhere. Those with small gardens should keep it in pots as it has very invasive tendencies. Propagate by division or sowing seeds in spring, or from cuttings in the growing season.
■ **MEDICINAL USES** Inhale drops of spearmint essential oil to help relieve colds. Drink infusions of peppermint tea to aid digestion.
■ **CULINARY USES** Spearmint is the type most used in cooking to flavour both sweet and savoury dishes and drinks.

Monarda didyma
BERGAMOT

Nepeta cataria
CATMINT

Ocimum basilicum
SWEET BASIL

Origanum vulgare
OREGANO/WILD MARJORAM

Pelargonium graveolens
ROSE GERANIUM

The fresh orangey smell, toothed oval leaves and striking pink or purple flowers make this a most attractive perennial that reaches 1 m/3 ft. It was brought to Europe from North America in the sixteenth century.

■ **CULTIVATION** Plant bergamot in light moist soil where it gets the morning sun. Propagate by taking root cuttings and planting out in late spring.
■ **MEDICINAL USES** Bergamot tea relieves insomnia, menstrual pain and nausea.
■ **CULINARY USES** Add to China tea for an Earl Grey flavour. The flowers can be used as a salad garnish.

An attractive member of the nettle family, this perennial grows to 1 m/3 ft and bears lavender blue flowers all summer. Its extraordinary scent, which is a combination of mint and pennyroyal, fascinates cats, who will roll in it, making the bruised leaves exude the smell.

■ **CULTIVATION** Sow seeds in autumn in a sunny spot.
■ **MEDICINAL USES** Catmint induces sleep and causes perspiration, so it is useful for treating fevers. Drink an infusion before going to bed. Make a poultice of the fresh leaves to relieve painful swellings.
■ **CULINARY USES** Use young leaves in salads.

A native of India, basil is a tender annual in cooler climes. With an abundance of large bright green leaves, it reaches 45 cm/18 in.

■ **CULTIVATION** Sow seeds indoors in spring. Plant out in a sunny position in well-drained soil after all danger of frost is passed. Slugs and snails love basil, so place gravel around its roots to prevent them reaching the leaves.
■ **MEDICINAL USES** Basil tea aids digestion.
■ **CULINARY USES** A delicious herb used liberally in Mediterranean cooking to make sauces, garnish salads and flavour pizzas and cooked vegetables.

Oregano grows freely on the hills of its native Greece, and its sweet spicy aroma gave it its name: *oros ganos*, or "joy-of-the-mountain". Oregano comes from a large family of plants and is covered in pointed oval leaves.

■ **CULTIVATION** Sow seeds under cover in autumn. Plant in rich soil in full sun with midday shade in spring. Cut back by two-thirds in autumn.
■ **MEDICINAL USES** An infusion relieves the symptoms of colds and coughs.
■ **CULINARY USES** Oregano is used in strongly flavoured Mediterranean and Mexican dishes. It combines well with chilli, garlic and tomatoes.

A tender perennial, green at first but later develops woody bark. Grows up to 1.2m/4 ft and produces small, pale pink flowers.

■ **CULTIVATION** Sow seeds indoors in spring, or take cuttings in late summer and plant out the following summer in dry soils and full sun. Cut plants down in autumn and cover with straw where light frost is possible.
■ **MEDICINAL USES** Geranium oil and geranium water are important in cosmetics. Oil distilled from the leaves can also act as an insect repellent.
■ **CULINARY USES** Rose-scented leaves are used to scent desserts, cakes and teas, and hot and cold drinks.

Petroselinum crispum
PARSLEY

Rosa
ROSE

Rosmarinus officinalis
ROSEMARY

Rumex acetosa
SORREL

Ruta graveolens
RUE

A popular biennial herb with finely cut and curled leaves, it reaches 38 cm/15 in.

■ **CULTIVATION** Plant in moist soil in a partially shaded position. Cut the leaves as you need them, as this will promote new growth. If the leaves become coarse, cut them down to encourage new young leaves. In its second year, parsley is quick to flower. Cut the flower stems down as soon as they appear to encourage leaf growth.
■ **MEDICINAL USES** Parsley tea is diuretic. Decoct the roots as a remedy for kidney troubles.
■ **CULINARY USES** Parsley should be used generously to flavour vegetables, sauces, egg, fish and tomato dishes.

There are rambling, climbing, shrub and miniature roses, with single or double blooms in numerous shades. Some have a single flowering period, others repeat through the season.

■ **CULTIVATION** Plant in rich soil in a sheltered position with light shade. Dead-head repeat-flowering roses regularly. Once-flowering roses sometimes have decorative hips, so leave the dead heads on the shrub.
■ **MEDICINAL USES** Essential oil used in aromatherapy soothes tension. Essential oil and petals are useful for cosmetic preparations.
■ **CULINARY USES** Crystallized petals make delightful decorations for sweets and puddings. Rosehips make a refreshing tea.

An evergreen shrub with needle-like leaves and blue flowers which appear in early summer. It becomes very bushy and can reach a height of 2 m/ 6 ft if not controlled.

■ **CULTIVATION** Propagate from seeds sown in spring, or from semi-ripe cuttings in summer. Plant in a sunny position in a sheltered spot in light, dry soil. Prune back in autumn.
■ **MEDICINAL USES** Oil of rosemary used in aromatherapy can ease headaches and general tension. An infusion used as a hair rinse controls dandruff and makes the hair shine.
■ **CULINARY USES** The leaves provide a pungent flavour for lamb, pork, potatoes and fish.

A leggy perennial reaching 1.2 m/4 ft, bearing large oval leaves and subtle reddish flowers that resemble large seeds.

■ **CULTIVATION** Plant seed in sun or light shade in spring and water well to keep leaves succulent. In autumn, cut the plant down and protect from frost with a cloche.
■ **MEDICINAL USES** Apply an infusion of sorrel to relieve mouth ulcers and boils. Drink the infusion to treat ailing kidneys and livers.
■ **CULINARY USES** Use the young leaves to make a fresh-tasting spring soup or sauce for fish, or add them to green salads.

This attractive blue-green plant can cause a photosensitive rash in some people that blisters in sunshine. The ancients considered it a powerful antidote to witchcraft and poison. A hardy evergreen sub-shrub, it reaches 60 cm/2 ft.

■ **CULTIVATION** A native of southern Europe, rue does best in poor soil in full sun. Wear gloves when handling.
■ **MEDICINAL USES** This plant should be used with extreme caution, only under supervision, and never during pregnancy. Traditionally, it was used to treat coughs, headaches, bronchitis, ulcers and wounds.
■ **CULINARY USES** Rue has a very bitter taste, and so is rarely used.

Salvia officinalis
SAGE

Sambucus nigra
COMMON ELDER

Sanguisorba officinalis
SALAD BURNET

Symphytum officinale
COMFREY

Tanacetum parthenium
FEVERFEW

The grey-green leaves, set in pairs, and blue flowers on this perennial shrub make it an attractive border plant that reaches a height of 60 cm/2 ft. Its name comes from the Latin *salvere*, which means "to cure".

■ **CULTIVATION** In spring sow seeds in full sun in light, dry soil. Cut back after flowering.

■ **MEDICINAL USES** Sage tea reduces fevers and is beneficial in liver and kidney complaints. Two drops of essential oil added to a bowl of hot water make a good inhalant to disperse heavy mucus.

■ **CULINARY USES** The strongly flavoured leaves are excellent for stuffings for meat and poultry. The flowers make a pretty addition to salads.

A deciduous shrub or small tree bearing fragrant blossoms and juicy dark purple berries.

■ **CULTIVATION** In spring sow seeds in fertile, moist soil in a sunny spot. Encourage bushiness by cutting all shoots down to the ground in winter. Alternatively, prune out all old wood and cut new growth to half.

■ **MEDICINAL USES** Ointment made from elder leaves relieves bruises and sprains. Elderberry wine was used to relieve a sore throat, shivering and fever at the onset of influenza.

■ **CULINARY USES** Elderflowers make delicious summer drinks. The berries are used to make wine, jam and chutney.

A most decorative plant with feathery leaves and green pom-pom flowers speckled with red. A hardy perennial, it is often grown as a border plant and it reaches 75 cm/30 in.

■ **CULTIVATION** In autumn or spring sow seeds in limy soil in a sunny spot. Harvest young leaves when you need them and prune off old leaves and flowers as they die to promote new leaf growth.

■ **MEDICINAL USES** Salad burnet is mildly diuretic and settles diarrhoea. It also eases sunburn.

■ **CULINARY USES** The subtle nutty flavour is useful for flavouring fish, cheeses, butters and salad.

This decorative perennial grows into a showy bush up to 1.2m/ 4 ft high, producing generous tapering leaves that become smaller the higher they are up the plant. From early summer, each stem is draped with a row of charming blue, purple, pink or creamy yellow bells. It can be poisonous and so should not be taken internally unless under professional supervision.

■ **CULTIVATION** Sow seeds in a sunny position in rich soil in autumn or spring. Fertilize monthly. Comfrey grows quite large and can be invasive. It can be difficult to eradicate.

■ **MEDICINAL USES** Roots or leaves can be used as a poultice to help reduce swelling and heal wounds.

■ **CULINARY USES** None.

A member of the chrysanthemum family, feverfew has a charming daisy-like flower and delicate cut leaves. A hardy perennial, it reaches 60 cm/2 ft in height.

■ **CULTIVATION** Sow seeds in spring or autumn in a sunny position in well-drained soil, and feverfew will come up year after year.

■ **MEDICINAL USES** Spring leaves can be made into a sandwich to disguise the bitter taste and eaten daily to relieve chronic migraine. In winter, dried feverfew can be substituted, but it is not as effective. Feverfew also helps to relieve arthritis.

■ **CULINARY USES** Feverfew's bitter taste is not suitable for flavouring food.

Taraxacum officinale
DANDELION

The deeply indented leaves of this familiar wild flower give it its common name, taken from the French *dent de lion*, meaning "lion's tooth".

■ **CULTIVATION** Generally considered to be a weed, it can be found in most gardens. The deep tap root is perennial and difficult to remove. Harvest it when it is two years old.

■ **MEDICINAL USES** An infusion of dandelion leaves is an efficient diuretic that is rich in potassium, making it an excellent treatment for urinary infections. Make a decoction of dandelion root to stimulate the liver – excellent for treating jaundice or a malfunctioning gall-bladder.

■ **CULINARY USES** Dandelion leaves can be used in salads.

Thymus pseudolanuginosus
(woolly thyme)
THYME

This vast family of evergreen aromatic herbs comes in many forms, with leaves ranging from yellow through blue-green to silver. Some are fine, almost needle-like, others are broad. Some are smooth and glossy, others are hairy. Flowers can be white, pink or purple. There are three general types: the bushy thymes reaching 35cm/ 14 in; the mat-forming thymes which reach only 5 cm/2 in; and those that form a low hummock, between the two heights. Its most potent constituent, thymol, a powerful antiseptic, was first isolated in 1725.

Thymus x *citriodorus* 'Aureus'
(lemon-scented golden variegated thyme)

■ **CULTIVATION** Thyme likes to be planted in well-drained limy soil in an open sunny position. In late summer, after flowering, clip back to encourage a compact bushy habit. If left straggly, thyme is more likely to die in the winter.

■ **MEDICINAL USES** An infusion of thyme aids catarrh and sore throats, and promotes perspiration at the beginning of a cold. Used as a mouthwash, the natural antiseptic in thyme will ease ulcers and gum infections.

■ **CULINARY USES** Thyme is an essential ingredient of bouquet garnis, used to flavour soups, casseroles, meat and vegetable dishes.

Trifolium pratense
RED CLOVER

With a pink pom-pom flower and leaf divided into three segments, this short-lived perennial grows up to 60 cm/ 2 ft high. It has been important since the middle ages as a forage crop.

■ **CULTIVATION** A hardy plant that grows easily in light sandy soil.

■ **MEDICINAL USES** The antiseptic quality of red clover makes it a good mouthwash for throat infections.

■ **CULINARY USES** None.

Tropaeolum majus
NASTURTIUM

A twining climber with bright orange, yellow or red flowers and round leaves. The name comes from the Latin *nasus tortus* ("contorted nose"), referring to its pungent smell. Nasturtiums are among the most easily grown hardy annuals.

■ **CULTIVATION** Plant seed in well-drained soil in a sunny position. Flowers will appear from mid- to late summer.

■ **MEDICINAL USES** Rub bruised leaves over the face to clear spots and blemishes.

■ **CULINARY USES** Flowers and leaves make a piquant and pretty addition to salads. Fresh seeds are good in salads, too.

Viola tricolor

HEARTSEASE/WILD PANSY

A charming miniature yellow and blue pansy, the parent of many larger varieties developed since Victorian times. A short-lived perennial, it is usually grown as an annual.

■ **CULTIVATION** Easy to grow in almost any soil, water when the topsoil feels dry to the touch. Dead-head regularly to encourage further blooms.

■ **MEDICINAL USES** Make an infusion of the flowers as a laxative, a decoction of the leaves to ease catarrh.

■ **CULINARY USES** Used mainly for decoration in salads and on sweets and desserts.

RIGHT *A traditional herb garden with alliums in the foreground.*

SOURCES AND ACKNOWLEDGEMENTS

My special thanks go to Polly, whose glorious photographs have made the book a visual delight; to Helen, who so skilfully and calmly steered the subject of herbs into fresh fields; to Sara Lewis whose recipes are as delicious as they are pretty; to Mr and Mrs Cho for letting us photograph in their most graceful house; to Judith and Simon Hopkinson of Hollington Nurseries, Rosemary Titterington of Iden Croft Herbs and Christine Forecast of Congham Hall Hotel, all of whom allowed us to photograph in their herb gardens; to David Roberts, Head Gardener at Congham Hall, for sharing his herbal knowledge; to Caroline Cilia for assisting me so enthusiastically on some of the sessions.

CONGHAM HALL
COUNTRY HOUSE
HOTEL,
Linn Road,
Grimston,
King's Lynn,
Norfolk PE32 1AH.
Tel: 01485 600250.
A delightful country hotel whose kitchen garden now contains 600 varieties that are used in the kitchen.

DAMASK,
3-4 Broxholme
House,
Harwood Road,
London SW6 4AA.
Tel: 0171 731 3553.
Beautiful linens, lavender and rose bags, herb prints.

HOLLINGTON
NURSERIES,
Woolton Hill,
Newbury,
Berkshire RG15 9XT.
Tel: 01635 253908.
Several beautifully laid-out herb gardens, a nursery and herbs to buy. Small gift shop and tea rooms.

HOP SHOP,
Castle Farm,
Shoreham,
Sevenoaks,

Kent TN14 7UB.
Tel: 01959 523219.
Hop and dried flower growers. They supply fresh and dried hop bines and dried flowers.

IDEN CROFT HERBS,
Frittenden Road,
Staplehurst,
Kent TN12 0DH.
Tel: 01580 891432.
Prettily laid-out herb gardens, nursery and herbs to buy. Gift shop and tea rooms.

NORFOLK
LAVENDER,
Caley Mill,
Heacham,
King's Lynn,
Norfolk PE31 7JE.
Tel: 01485 570384.
Growers and suppliers (inc. mail order) of lavender plants and dried lavender, plus lavender products. Lavender fields, guided tours, gift shop and tea room.

THE ROMANTIC
GARDEN NURSERY,
Swannington,
Norwich,
Norfolk NR9 5NW.
Tel: 01603 261488.
Topiary.

AUSTRALIA

RENAISSANCE HERBS,
Head Office Tel:
943 93 1221.
*Wholesale growers
operating in all
states with a large
variety of potted
herbs.*

HOUSE OF HERBS,
1 Digney Street,
Sandy Bay,
Tasmania 7005.
Tel: 018 146576.
*Sells potted herbs,
home-made soaps,
cosmetics, and other
herbal products.*

TLC HERBS,
Lot 10,
Old Coach Road,
Aldinga ASA 5173.
Tel: 085 577 161.
*Sells potted and cut
fresh herbs. Formal
herb garden.*

THURLBY HERB
FARM,
Gardiner Road,
Walpole WA6 398.
Tel: 098402 249.
*Large range of
herbal projects,
cosmetics, culinary
and crafts.*

RESOURCE
INFORMATION
*For information on
any aspect of the
herb industry in
Australia, the
Australian Herb
Industry Resource
Guide by Kim
Fletcher is
invaluable. Regularly
updated.
Available from*
FOCUS ON HERBS
CONSULTANCY &
INFORMATION
SERVICE,
PO Box 203,

Launcestron,
Tasmania 7250.
Tel: 003 301 493.

FRAGRANT HERB
COTTAGE,
Cnr Lemke &
Roghan Roads,
Taigum,
Brisbane,
Qld 4018.
Tel: 07 3216 2422.
*Large range of herbs
and herbal products.*

BUNDANOON
VILLAGE NURSERY,
71 Penrose Road,
Bundanoon,
NSW.
Tel: 048 83 6303.
*Specializes in plants
and seeds of culinary
herbs, old books and
herbals.*

ROYAL BOTANIC
GARDENS,
Mrs Macquarie's
Road,
Sydney 2000.
Tel: 02 231 8111.
*Herb garden has a
wide range of herbs
used for culinary,
flavouring, aromatic,
medicinal purposes.*

AYLWEN'S HERBARY,
Cupacumbalong
Homestead,
Naas Road,
Tharwa ACT 2620.
Tel: 06 237 5277.
*Over 500 potted
herbs sold, plus
display gardens.*

HERBAGE HERB
GARDEN AND
NURSERY,
3 Gent Street,
Ballarat,
Vic 3350.
Tel: 053 326 412.
*Herb plants and
seeds for sale and by
mail order.*

INDEX